Science and technology are not only crucial but also paradoxical forces behind societal change. Societies depend on science and technology to solve social problems, but their contributions are often also controversial. The series of publications entitled 'Wissenschafts- und Techikforschung' (Science and Technology Studies) provides a forum in which these developments can be investigated in different dimensions, with a focus on sociology, philosophy, social anthropology and history. The series provides both foundational knowledge in all scientific disciplines as well as guidelines for decision makers and all those interested in this subject area.

Series
„Wissenschafts- und Technikforschung"
NEUE FOLGE

Edited by
Prof. Dr. Stefan Böschen, RWTH Aachen, Germany
Prof. Dr. Gabriele Gramelsberger, RWTH Aachen, Germany
Prof. Dr. Jörg Niewöhner, HU Berlin, Germany
Prof. Dr. Heike Weber, TU Berlin, Germany

Up to Volume 18 edited by:
Prof. Dr. Alfons Bora, Bielefeld University, Germany
Prof. Dr. Sabine Maasen, TU Munich, Germany
Prof. Dr. Carsten Reinhardt, Bielefeld University, Germany
PD Dr. Peter Wehling, University of Frankfurt am Main, Germany

Volume 24

Albena Vutsova | Todor Yalamov
Martina Arabadzhieva

In Search of Excellent Research Assessment

The Deutsche Nationalbibliothek lists this publication in the
Deutsche Nationalbibliografie; detailed bibliographic data
are available on the Internet at http://dnb.d-nb.de

ISBN 978-3-8487-7587-3 (Print)
      978-3-7489-3720-3 (ePDF)

British Library Cataloguing-in-Publication Data
A catalogue record for this book is available from the British Library.

ISBN 978-3-8487-7587-3 (Print)
      978-3-7489-3720-3 (ePDF)

Library of Congress Cataloging-in-Publication Data
Albena Vutsova | Todor Yalamov | Martina Arabadzhieva
In Search of Excellent Research Assessment
Vutsova, Albena | Yalamov, Todor | Arabadzhieva, Martina
176 pp.
Includes bibliographic references.

ISBN 978-3-8487-7587-3 (Print)
      978-3-7489-3720-3 (ePDF)

edition sigma in the Nomos Verlagsgesellschaft

1st Edition 2023
© The Authors
Published by
Nomos Verlagsgesellschaft mbH & Co. KG
Waldseestraße 3–5 | 76530 Baden-Baden
www.nomos.de

Production of the printed version:
Nomos Verlagsgesellschaft mbH & Co. KG
Waldseestraße 3–5 | 76530 Baden-Baden

ISBN 978-3-8487-7587-3 (Print)
ISBN 978-3-7489-3720-3 (ePDF)
DOI   https://doi.org/10.5771/9783748937203

Onlineversion
Nomos eLibrary

This work is licensed under a Creative Commons Attribution
4.0 International License.

Acknowledgments

The authors would like to extend their gratitude to the following people, who contributed significantly to the book:

- Dr. Todor Hristov, Sofia University "St. Kliment Ohridski", Bulgaria
- Dr. Ing. Leos Hornicek, Head Office, Czech Academy of Sciences, Czech Republic
- Dr. Tsvetelina Dimitrova, Bikam Plus Ltd, Bulgaria
- Dr. Radostina Angelova, Global Metrics Bulgaria Ltd, Bulgaria
- Dr. Stefan Radev, Apex Group Ltd, Bulgaria
- Dr. Snezhina Gabova, Research & Training Point Foundation, Bulgaria
- Dr. Micheal Ochsner, leader of WG 1, COST Action 15 137 "European Network for Research Evaluation in the Social Sciences and the Humanities", ETH Zurich & FORS Lausanne, Switzerland
- Mrs. Rumyana Muhtarova, Sofia TechPark, Bulgaria
- Mrs. Marina Arnaudova, British Council – Sofia, Bulgaria
- Mrs. Vanya Grashkina, Director of the National Centre for Information and Documentation, Bulgaria
- Zhelyaz Enev, Ministry of Economy and Industry, Bulgaria
- Samuel Jezny, Ministry of Education, Youth and Sports, Czech Republic

This work was supported by the project "Building Scientific Capacity through Knowledge Transfer, Exchange of Hands-on Practices, Linked Academic Research and Networking" (SCHOLARNET).

Table of Contents

Introduction and context	9
I. Research Evaluation: What, Why, Who?	19
1. Research evaluation in perspective	19
2. History	21
3. Research evaluation: tasks	26
4. Types of research evaluation	30
5. Evaluation procedures based on scientometrics	40
6. Bibliometric indicators	41
6.1. Evaluation procedures based on expert conclusions	48
6.2. Socio-economic models for research evaluation	48
6.3. New research evaluation methods	50
7. Ethics in research evaluation	53
References	60
II. Research Impact Assessment	69
1. Impact assessment – General definition	69
2. The assessment of scientific research and its impact on higher education systems and horizontal research organisations	75
2.1. Importance of research assessment for universities	75
3. Methods for assessing research impact	77
4. Social impact of research	84
5. Practical comments	88
References	89
III. Main Methodologies	95
References	108

Table of Contents

IV. Comparing research assessment models on a national level — 111
    1. Is there a common European model? — 112
    2. The Anglo-Saxon research assessment model — 114
    3. National research assessment practices in EU Member States — 116
        3.1. Austria — 117
        3.2. The Netherlands — 120
        3.3. Czech Republic — 124
        3.4. Hungary — 127
        3.5. Bulgaria — 130
        3.6. Poland — 134
        3.7. Lithuania — 137
        3.8. Slovenia — 139
    4. Main research assessment indicators influencing the innovation ecosystem — 143
    5. Participation in partnership networks — 159
    References — 161

V. Concluding reflection and forward looking — 167
    References: — 174

List of authors — 175

Introduction and context

Reflection serves as a circulation system for philosophy and a backbone for epistemology. Locke (1689) explores human understanding through the different manifestations of reflection – perceiving, thinking, doubting, believing, reasoning, knowing and willing. Reflection of scientific activity has evolved over the years from complete agnostics or relative doubts in the methods and integrity of individual researchers into comprehensive systems of science evaluation against sets of priorities and budgets. One may argue that this specific reflection was transformed from individual will and reasoning into an instrument of power.

The institutionalisation of science evaluation is intertwined with the development of the audit culture (Shore and Wright, 1999). The audit culture is viewed very differently from liberal and leftist perspectives. While the liberals would see audit culture as a progress in democratic governance, the leftists would see it as a strengthening of the status-quo and an instrument to control independent thinking.

Objectively, audit practices are a set of actions and control processes that are carried out by authorised control bodies within the framework of collected and analysed financial and non-financial information for the purpose of assessing the management of financial resources and the accountability of stakeholders with a view to achieving a potential improvement of the process.

It is a common belief that scientific audits and open science make science more transparent and thus more efficient in context of informing better policy decisions. Reichmann and Weiser's (2022) reflection on the science-policy relationships sheds doubt if deeper scrutiny is needed on the science part, but instead advocate widening of policy-making process. Policymakers seek information that is timely, relevant, credible, and available. Audit practices might and could contribute to these ends, however not without participatory engagement in policymaking.

Auditing has proliferated in virtually all spheres of social and economic life, not just the accounting and financial fields. It goes hand in hand with the emergence of new standards (i.e., environmental) and rising compliance costs.

Auditing practices have deep historical roots – from managing the relationship between landlords and peasants to modern corporations with dispersed ownership. Auditing is rooted in the need to have a sound system of checks and balances and perform various control activities. Independent auditing emerged and became increasingly sought after in the late nineteenth century. The United Kingdom, France, Germany, Italy, the Netherlands and Austria were among the first to impose legal regulations on this activity. Auditing was professionalised out of the need to guarantee that managers of corporations do not harm the interests of the state and those of the stakeholders. Classical financial audits were enhanced with performance audits as it became easier to manipulate the accounts over time.

Simultaneously, universities evolved significantly from a typical guild organisation (Medieval Bologna and Paris) the sole purpose of which is to produce educated people. They grew in number and size, changed the way recruitment of professors was performed (in 11th century it was the students' guild that appointed professors based on reputation and not on formal qualifications) and how universities were governed (a top-down corporate approach or bottom-up cooperative self-governance). The Bologna process, which was initiated in 1999, specifically focused on quality assurance as an integration instrument among different national higher education systems and individual European universities. For some observers quality assurance might come at the expense of academic freedom and independence, a former priority of the Bologna Declaration from 1988 (the Magna Charta Universitatum).

The "Standards and Guidelines for Quality Assurance in the European Higher Education Area"[1] was adopted in 2005, and was revised in 2015 by the European ministers of education. Although the standards were not meant to be applied to research per se, they do reflect the relationship between research and education Moreover, the underlying principles of quality assurance are the same as in every audit process and research evaluation, or to put it in a more abstract way – in every professionalised organised reflection: independence, objectivity, confidentiality, integrity and responsibility for the opinion expressed.

So, research evaluation developed together with the spread of the audit culture and accelerated due to integrative demands within the world of

---

1 http://www.ehea.info/media.ehea.info/file/2015_Yerevan/72/7/European_Standards_and_Guidelines_for_Quality_Assurance_in_the_EHEA_2015_MC_613727.pdf

higher education in the European Union. First in Britain in the early 1990s and then followed by other European countries, the elite higher education started to engage wider audiences expecting to reach half of secondary education graduates. Increasing the share of people with higher education is set as one of the main aims in the program documents of the EU. The Bologna process expanded the base by transforming the system of Fachhochshules (Germany, Austria, Cyprus and others) into universities of applied sciences which award bachelor and master degrees.

New universities flourished also in Eastern European countries after the political changes in 1989. The students enrolled in tertiary education in the EU have risen 1.5 times between 2000 and 2020, according to the World Bank data/UNESCO Institute of Statistics. Higher education institutions in Europe also mark increase in numbers, especially in new member states and associated countries during the last two decades (European Education and Culture Executive Agency, Eurydice, 2020).

These trends were accompanied by vast diversification of new educational programs and growing concerns about the overall quality of education. The new universities (often wrongly called red brick universities, as the term originated only for the civic universities in XIX century England) embraced the evaluation processes to increase public confidence. Yet, in certain countries the evaluation processes turned out to be highly bureaucratised and resulted in a self-replicating system.

So, when assessing the research assessments one should employ a cost-benefit approach. Do research assessments add value? To whom? Who pays the costs associated with them? Are they just a public cost, a fraction of all public investments in education and research or they are paid unevenly by some sub-group of researchers and universities?

The difference in academic and political "cultures" and "languages", including the typical time-frames (longer horizons for researchers), knowledge and facts, even reputation mechanics, create a niche opportunity, where the evaluation practices, in various scope and format, could provide what both parties are looking for (Reichmann & Wieser, 2022).

At the same time research evaluation, as well as quality assurance in a larger higher education context, emerged as additional markets and source of income for key stakeholders of the system which is being evaluated. The current book studies this specific quasi-market of research/scientific assessments from diverse institutional perspectives. A contextual issue which drives our explorations is the complex relationship between the diffusion of audit culture in universities and the quality and interoperability of universities across different countries. The main institutional driver for that market is the Bologna process with the synchronization of bachelor, master and doctoral degrees, as well the standardisation of accreditation agencies to a certain degree.

Evaluation practices are relevant and additive, to a large extent, to the principles of good governance: openness, participation, accountability, efficiency, ethics and reasonable financial management, etc. The concept of governance is understood in many ways by different people. Its definition often depends on the objectives pursued, the actors involved and the socio-political environment in which these objectives are to be achieved, but the principles remain essentially unchanged.

Taking the position that the main mission of evaluation is to improve the internal research process, it can be further extrapolated that evaluation can be and is a necessary condition for the subsequent growth of international mechanisms, in which it is postulated that competitiveness is the first requirement to have access to financial instruments.

Historically, the development of research was initially supported only by wealthy individuals, churches or national resources and the issue of evaluation and control did not dominate the development policy. At a later stage, however, other financial flows in support of research entered – second and third – and were implemented either on a project-based competitive basis or at the request of a donor or creator.

After the second half of the last century, research evaluations developed and diversified. Not only did they have different goals, but they were aimed at different levels – local, national, transnational, that is. regional), European, trans-European. If one looks only at one type of evaluations or assessment, it would be difficult to understand or meta-assess its applicability and usability. Therefore, a comparative analysis of different evaluations would help us to better understand the very nature of the process, the motivations of those involved and the impact on the system.

At the beginning of the 1990s, all of the new EU member states were still implementing a science policy and evaluation mechanisms that were a continuation or a replica of the ones in the USSR. The Soviet audit culture in universities was exactly what Shore and Wright (1999) were referring to – a political structure for staff control, which assured a patronised career development nurtured by the party favouring loyal professors. The political institutionalisation was in the form of higher attestation committees (or VAKs), which had the power – the upper chamber – to stop or further any career development despite the assessment of the lower chamber.

The academic landscape was sharply divided in two parts – higher education institutions and universities, which were mainly educationally-oriented, and the centralised academies of sciences which only focused on doing pure research without including an educational component. Of course, there were various diffusions between the respective groups, which led to some institutional integration in the mid to late 1980s (at least in the case of Bulgaria).

The liquidation of the VAKs, followed by the decentralization of the career development system for scholars took place at the beginning of the new century. The effect was sometimes controversial, because the desire for a rapid career growth in the field of research, combined with personal assessment systems, which were not always sufficiently demanding, reflected on the quality of work and, in some cases, on the devaluation of certain research positions. Regardless of some imperfections, however, it is very important that the new system, which copies European practices in its main part, guarantees relative academic freedom and that independent evaluators, in the form of juries, are neither political bodies, nor politically engaged.

The assessment criteria that were applied were largely typified, following international trends, but they were not sustainable over time. They were often influenced by sporadic "modern trends" that were introduced quickly, without analysis and evaluation of the impact, which sometimes led to quite unpleasant consequences. Then they would disappear, but the inherited problems would remain much longer.

The introduction of a criteria-based objective system regarding the assessment of research organisations was also influenced by the manifest accreditation system of Great Britain (at that time it was a European practice, and Great Britain was a member of the EU). Accountability to society, imposed by Margaret Thatcher as a result of the outcomes of the white paper on education, was very well received in almost all member states and membership candidates. This seemed reasonable because public funds were being spent. National Accreditation Agencies, which have a similar mission, almost identical criteria that were largely a replica of the British system, were formed over a short period of time in the countries.

The EU agencies themselves are quite different, because education and science policies are horizontal policies and, therefore, full synchronization is not expected.

For example, for Germany, the applicable criteria for research assessment as part of general accreditation include individual achievements in teaching, writing proposals or adequately recognised publications. Performance evaluation is not limited to merely counting the number of publications or comparing index factors. Performance evaluation should primarily be based on qualitative standards. The assessment of a researcher's achievement must be carried out in its entirety and must be based on substantive qualitative criteria. In addition to the publication of articles, books, data and software, other dimensions can be taken into account, such as involvement in teaching, academic self-administration, public relations or knowledge and technology transfer. Details of quantitative metrics such as impact factors and h-indices are not required and are not to be considered as part of the review. Accreditation focuses on curricula (assessed for quality), research is not an explicit object of this assessment, although it is presented as a criterion.

For other countries – for example Bulgaria – the number of publications in indexed journals is a leading criterion for assessing the quality of research activity.

Another factor that strongly influences the evaluation process in Eastern European countries is the Tempus program – conceived as a program for the modernization of higher education. Initially, it was identified as part of the PHARE program. This program started as targeted aid to Poland and Hungary, then expanded to other countries in Central and Eastern Europe. Subsequently, Tempus was distinguished as a separate program (it has three execution cycles).

During the implementation of the Tempus program in the CEE countries, almost all projects involved old member countries, which were often also leading a given project, and their good practices were easily transferred to the new member countries, the same applies to the evaluation process.

In support of these assertions, we also offer the case study of the establishment of an accreditation agency in Bulgaria. The project under PHARE-BG 95.06 – 05.01.001.: the first phase "Preliminary study for accreditation of higher education institutions in Bulgaria" was implemented with the consulting support of the Center for Quality Support at the Free University of London (Quality Support Centre, Open University-London-QSC) with long-term experts Prof. William Callaway (November 1996 – May 1997) and Dr. Hugh Glenville, and its second phase "National Assessment and Accreditation Agency" was implemented over the course of one year by a British Council team led by Dr. D. Billing. Pilot accreditations of higher education institutions were also carried out. Thus, PHARE was an instrument for the early transfer of the British audit culture in Bulgaria.

The superimposition of crisis factors determines a number of peculiarities in the introduction of institutional accreditation. The first and perhaps the most essential feature is the shift of the focus of evaluation from development to accountability by limiting the procedure to seek compliance with state requirements. Another feature is the emphasis on accreditation instead of the process of self-evaluation by the institution and evaluation by external experts. Although the decision to accredit an institution is the result of an assessment, by the very nature of accreditation for both assessees and assessors the focus is on the outcome (i.e., recognition of compliance with laws and government requirements and the granting of a license to continue the activity) rather than on the process itself (i.e., the quality of the assessment). This becomes even more important due to the fact that the refusal to accredit an institution according to the regulations leads to severe sanctions, including closure, which happens very rarely.

While major industry evaluations (i.e. ISO-related) are process-oriented, many research evaluations are centred around the outcomes of the system. Even when process evaluation is immanently a part of the overall evaluation it has a somewhat lower priority than the must-have outcomes.

In some cases, the development of institutional accreditation has been dictated by the widely shared perception that the unsatisfactory state of higher education is primarily due to its structural inefficiency. Therefore, it is assumed that with the improvement of the general structure of the system, more favourable conditions should be created for improving the quality of teaching and scientific research. In order to achieve this, a number of national, European and trans-European financial instruments have been introduced to help solve this problem. This process is not new at all. At the very beginning of the transition to a market economy in some of the countries of central Europe – former satellites of the USSR, grant schemes were awarded through the World Bank to solve some of the problems of the research system and, more precisely, of higher education. Subsequently, almost all EU candidate countries implemented similar projects with the financial support of the World Bank. In a very large part of them, the emphasis was placed on the modernization of the higher education process, its assessment and convergence with good international practices.

All such tools have an effect on the research environment to varying degrees. But in all cases, it (research environment) is influenced and respectively responsive to intervention and leads to behavioural changes.

However, the changes in behaviour as a result of the changes in the research environment have led to a lack of trust in it and, in turn, in the research guild. (Dis)trust and (dis)respect are considered among the most important factors for research update (Oliver et al. 2014). Therefore, it can be assumed that one of the reasons for introducing new formal criteria is to improve the image of researchers, and for them to use it as a "label" or sign of quality, implying some kind of prestige and the possibility of comparability with other renowned researchers. In a similar context, research institutions proposing similar indicators of comparability can also be compared.

Education and research are constantly being marketised. They are being considered as market products. This in turn results in a massification of education, leading to a decrease in its quality and an absence of a research component. As a consequence, this negatively affects the reputation of researchers involved in the education process. Therefore, a certain kind of "recognition" of researchers is also necessary in order to restore their reputation. The formal evaluation process could contribute to this end, if it includes international benchmarking and popular media.

In the social comparison theory, social competition is assumed to be an element of the framework of these comparisons. In a sense, the evaluative nature of research corresponds to this statement. Based on trivial criteria, certain institutions are divided into groups. They are typified by certain characteristics. In addition, the theory postulates that social motivation is the result of 5 factors, one of which is "affirmation in society". Therefore, the categories into which a given research structure falls, as a result of the evaluation process, contribute to its "appropriateness" and ensure a "respectable" place in society.

There is a global unabated debate on which universities do better than the others, which researchers are better than others, where to publish and, at the end of the day, how to evaluate and fund the research systems on a national level.

The answer to the latter has important consequences for the research behaviour of organisations and their members. Policymakers influence research output through the research evaluation systems they adopt, due to the fact they are strongly linked to the financial support provided to any given research organisation.

So, what is the best research evaluation system then? Does it exist at all? Is Europe converging or diverging on how countries evaluate their research systems? What are the contextual factors which will determine the institutional suitability of a given research evaluation system to a given national context? What is the subject of the evaluation – outcomes or the assessment process itself?

The anchor of this book or the underlying question is how and to what extent research evaluation practices are interrelated with the national innovation ecosystems. Would there be differences in small open economies, such as Bulgaria, the Czech Republic, Hungary, Lithuania, and Slovenia, or bigger ones, such as Poland, Austria, and the Netherlands? Why do some countries focus on qualitative and others on quantitative indicators? Why do some countries use holistic approaches and other use patchwork (copied fragments from different countries)? How can we link policy priorities, changes in the institutional framework, evaluation planning, and impact measuring in such turbulent times?

Furthermore, could we possibly find examples of practices of a research assessment, which is aligned with societal priorities (communicated through civil society organisations, NGOs) and not with political priorities which change every time there is a change in the political infrastructure? Böschen et al. (2020) advocate for the need for participatory research but also explore its challenges related to epistemic control. There are various examples of how civil society participates in the knowledge creation process in the same way as business representatives have been doing so for decades. The vast majority of research assessment literature, however, does not reflect the quality of research from a societal perspective.

We were curious to see if we could find a compromise between the two perspectives of audit culture from the beginning. The in-depth understanding of the academic landscape in Bulgaria and Eastern Europe suggests a possible third way of introducing an audit culture as an instrument of power within the academia.

The book's endeavour was partially motivated by the need to provide a somewhat coherent policy advice to the acceding countries from the Balkans. Nevertheless, we believe the findings, conclusions, and recommendations could be useful to CIS and BRICS countries as well. At the same time, all three authors have deep roots in civil society and we believe that the book could also assist in finding a way to achieve a larger civil society engagement in research assessment as a way to bypass the political control and self-iterating system of accreditation agencies and processes.

The book provides an analysis of the latest trends in research assessment systems worldwide and concrete methodologies applied by comparing eight European Union countries. Of course, in view of the fact that the authors are Bulgarian, their country might be overrepresented in examples, but it is only because it is most in need of policy actions among the eight national systems which are the subject of the study.

The book argues that the research assessment system and the national innovation system and the overall institutional enforcement are interdependent. Countries with better rule-of-law and a higher level of innovativeness tend to have more qualitative indicators and stronger peer-review, while those with weak governance systems, low public trust and a low level of innovativeness would prioritise quantitative and objective indicators, however with an overall lower quality than their counterparts.

Last but not least, the idea for the book emerged as a result of the excellent work on the *European Network for Research Evaluation in the Social Sciences and the Humanities* (COST Action 15137) project, which allowed for research assessment know-how to be shared and in which the leading author actively participated.

We hope that this study could serve as a powerful mirror for different stakeholders such as policymakers, research organisations, individual researchers who would wish to design new research evaluation initiatives, but also for think tanks and civil society activists.

Although many people have contributed to the book by providing documents, giving interviews, reading parts of the text, and providing comments and suggestions, all errors remain ours.

Böschen, S., Legris, M., Pfersdorf, S., & Stahl, B. C. (2020). Identity politics: Participatory research and its challenges related to social and epistemic control. *Social Epistemology*, 34(4), 382–394.

European Education and Culture Executive Agency, Eurydice, (2020). The European higher education area in 2020: Bologna process implementation report, Publications Office. https://data.europa.eu/doi/10.2797/756192

Locke, J. (1689) Essay concerning human understanding

Oliver, K., Innvar, S., Lorenc, T., Woodman, J., & Thomas, J. (2014). A systematic review of barriers to and facilitators of the use of evidence by policymakers. *BMC health services research*, 14, 1–12.

Reichmann, S., & Wieser, B. (2022). Open science at the science–policy interface: bringing in the evidence? *Health Research Policy and Systems*, 20(1), 1–12.

Shore, C., & Wright, S. (1999). Audit culture and anthropology: Neo-liberalism in British higher education. *Journal of the royal anthropological institute*, 557–575.

I. Research Evaluation: What, Why, Who?

1. Research evaluation in perspective

Research evaluation is still not a research field per se but rather an incorporated element in the creation of a new, contemporary, and competitive public value, which is often part of other evaluative procedures. Research evaluation seems to be rather a governance than a reflection instrument. However, research evaluation attracted a diversified interest of researchers around the globe in recent years. The total number of papers included in Web of Science Core Collection (WoSCC) mentioning *research evaluation* as a topic grew substantially faster than the database itself (118 % growth for research evaluation papers compared to 30 % growth for all papers in WoSCC for the period 2011–2021).

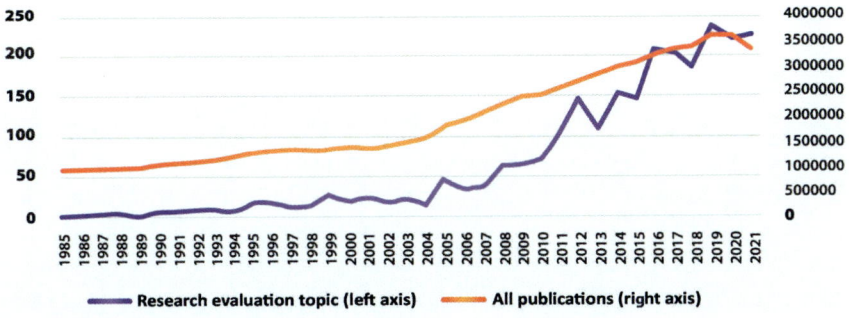

Source: Web of Science Core Collection (accessed February 12, 2022).

Figure 1.1: Growth of interest in publications on "research evaluation" (1985–2021)

The geography of authors publishing on research evaluation expanded with 41 new countries in the last 10 years. Among them are Poland and Bulgaria. In both countries the interest in research evaluation correlated with important policy debates, which lead to the new governance of research and innovation systems in the countries.

I. Research Evaluation: What, Why, Who?

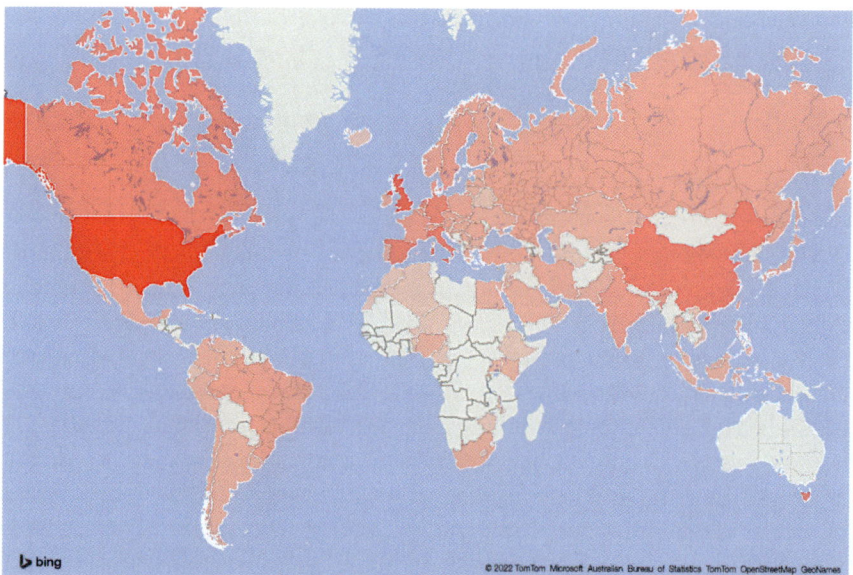

Source: Web of Science Core Collection (accessed February 12, 2022).

Figure 1.2: Frequency of publications with topic "research evaluation" by country (all time)

The Constitution for Science law in Poland adopted in 2018 significantly changed the evaluation criteria for research performance. As Michal Grabowski, head of department of invertebrate zoology and hydrobiology of the University of Lodz, put it in a recent interview, the law changed the value of an academic unit from "as good as its best scientist" to "as good as its worst scientist" (Zubascu, 2018). Papers by Polish authors constitute 5 % of all papers on the topic published in 2021 in Web of Science. The research policy shifts have different roots – from the pragmatic need to develop a research system which could deliver technology transfer services to local and international companies to the wish to have an instrument for a generational change especially in social sciences.

Fahrenkrog et al. (2002) defines evaluation as a "**systematic and objective process designed to assess the relevance and effectiveness of policies, programmes and projects**". Research evaluation emerged as a policy response to the need to justify budget spending for fundamental and applied research at universities and institutes. Initially resembling more a cost-benefit analysis, later it also became a policy design support tool, systematically gathering information on research performance on national, regional, institutional, or individual level.

2. History

Elements of research evaluation could be seen already at the beginning of the 20th century. As early as 1917, Frances J. Cole and Nelly B. Eels applied a quantitative analysis to comparative anatomy literature from 1543 to 1860. Their work was both descriptive and evaluative in nature. They used a curve to present the rate of document growth over the span of three centuries. They also indicated which aspects of the subject matter attracted researchers' interest in a given period of time (De Bellis, 2009).

The Vannevar Bush's 1945 report to the President of the United States contained a statement that quality control must be left to the internal mechanisms of the research elite using the peer review system. This model was then applied by the US National Science Foundation in 1947, and it was followed by other Western countries.

The first theme registers for scientific publications were created in the 50s and 60s. Soon after, the citation index developed by Eugene Garfield's Institute for Scientific Information was recognised as a way of objectifying research standards. Scientometrics has proven that it is possible to measure specific parameters regardless of some imperfections.

Marjanovic et al. (2009) indicates that one of the earliest studies in the field of evaluation, "The Sources of Invention" (Jewkes et al., 1958), has assessed 61 innovations in different scientific disciplines. This initiative was adopted by the US Department of Defence in 1967. It aimed to provide a justification for the size of the investments made in defence research (Sherwin & Isenson, 1967). Other studies examined back then the return on investment in research. Griliches (1958), for example, has evaluated the social norm for return on investment in hybrid corn-related studies.

Gibbons and Johnston (1974) have studied the role of scientific research in technological innovations and its contribution to industrial research and development. The authors have assessed 30 industrial innovations in Great Britain which include significant technological changes.

In 1968, The National Science Foundation conducted the TRACES study (Illinois Institute of Technology Research) and subsequently expanded this study via the Battelle project (Battelle Laboratories, 1973). It studied how 'non-mission oriented' research had contributed to the practical innovations. Battelle is best known for its nuclear research and involvement in the Manhattan project, but throughout the years it established itself as a premier centre for sustainable energy research and innovations.

The top two prolific contemporary authors on research evaluation are Giovanni Abramo and Ciriaco Andrea D'Angelo from the Laboratory for Studies of Research and Technology Transfer (LSRTT), Institute for System Analysis and Computer Science (IASI-CNR), National Research Council of Italy. They have, respectively, 61 and 58 papers (all of which co-authored with Abramo) on the topic in Web of Science Core Collection. The LSRTT school applies economics logic to production of research output, looks for alternatives of established indicators for scientific productivity, and studies the impact of national policies on publication behaviour, i.e. on self-citation behaviour (Abramo et al., 2021).

In research evaluation we find the so-called Hawthorne-like effect (Landsberger, 1958). It directly influences the behaviour of researchers. For instance, if you know you will be evaluated only on the basis of papers published in top journals, you might not publish elsewhere at all (and this could lead to higher turnover of non-tenured professors), and if you receive a bonus based on the number of papers, you may be prolific. If a lesser quality product requiring less efforts (i.e. a monograph of 101 pages published by whatever publishing house) would give you scores more than three times higher than a peer-review article in a Q1 journal, why you should rationally choose to work harder and taking the risk of several rejections? This is exactly the case of the current rules for academic promotion in Bulgaria.

Despite the differences in research evaluation metrics across Europe, there is a certain level of homogeneity of research evaluation systems. Research assessment systems are usually path-dependent – affected by historical, institutional, and political factors. Some countries with intensive research and scientific excellence (such as Netherlands, Austria, Switzerland, or Germany) apply less bibliometrics and more adaptive approaches, while others try to improve their ranking position by applying metrics and showing priority towards publications in English (Ochsner et al., 2018). Typically, research evaluation in post-communist countries is predominantly focused on the quantity rather than quality of publications (Jurajda et al., 2017), which is the case with Poland and Bulgaria as well.

The number of studies on the effects of specific research evaluation measures worldwide has increased significantly in the 1990s (Thomas et al., 2020). The relationships between science, technology, and markets are crucial for the market economy. Investments in scientific research are usually associated with high uncertainty – whether the research will lead to an invention of new technology, if the technology could be commercialised, and when these events will occur in time. In order to manage these risks, contemporary mechanisms for evaluating the effectiveness of scientific research have been developed.

Two important trends were observed in the last decade of the 20th century. The first was a shift in the understanding and assessment of research funding: grants perceived as part of the state's responsibility became investments with an expectation of economic efficiency. The second was a rise in the neoliberal approach to the value of knowledge, resulting in pressures to optimise and increase the efficiency[2] and intensity of scientific research. If knowledge is a commodity, then it should be produced by systems, subject to standardisation similar to other commodities (food, pharmaceutical products, cars, etc). Consequently, the mechanisms for evaluating scientific research were calibrated and became a key source of information in the decision-making process with regards to supporting research in the public sphere; public financing is provided on a competitive basis with results being measured on the basis of the generated added economic or social value (Leydesdorff, 2005). In the 1990s, the topic about measuring the impact of a given study attracted the attention of researchers (for example, Mansfield, 1991; Herbertz and Muller-Hill, 1995; Buxton and Hanney, 1996; Martin and Salter, 1996; Dawson et al., 1998; Hanney et al., 2003a, 2003b; Wooding et al., 2004b) and institutions which financed research.

Some changes were applied in the work process with regards to the approach to research evaluation and proof, leading to the creation of the San Francisco Declaration on Research Assessment (DORA), signed in 2013 and supported by 2,552 organisations and 19,126 people (last update: beginning of May 2022). The document offers recommendations targeted at financing organisations, research institutions, publishers, structures, which provide statistics, and researchers. The purpose of these recommendations is to correct the unforeseen effects triggered by the evaluation mechanisms established in the 1990s. In order to make the quality of research output measurable, these mechanisms have been adjusted to transform it into

---

2 The efficiency shows to what extent the goals set in a given programme have been achieved or whether they are on track of being reached (EC, 2017a).The analysis of effectiveness studies the relationship between the resources invested in a given intervention and the changes achieved (EC, 2017a).

quantitative indicators. Since 2013 this approach led to an intense growth in terms of quantity, which critics believe significantly surpasses the increase in the quality of the output.

On the other hand, since the quality of publications should be guaranteed via the peer review mechanisms created by scientific journals, the papers in such journals are privileged as opposed to monographs or publications in local or specialised issues. Apart from that, the quality of research publications is evaluated based on their impact which is calculated using different citation indices the coverage of which is limited due to the contents in databases which serve as the basis for calculations. The indicators also cover a limited amount of time because they set as a premise a relatively high speed of circulation of knowledge which does not account for the different rhythm of development of scientific disciplines.

In order to optimise the evaluation mechanisms for scientific research, the DORA authors recommend to mainly limit the use of metrics related to science journals, to encourage the evaluation of the research itself, not the editions in which it is published, and to use the advantages of online publishing (such as lack of limitations with regards to word count, figures and bibliography) and new indicators for measuring the significance and impact of research. It is noted that research outcomes can vary – new knowledge, data and software, or intellectual property, including well-trained young researchers. The authors believe that the impact of a given study on a specific policy or practice also represents a scientific impact indicator. Mentorship and societal engagement of researchers are other achievements which matter (Curry, 2018), and some of them are being evaluated. For instance, the Plymouth University in United Kingdom introduced Community Research Awards[3] in 2009, being a clear proof of social engagement of researchers.

The DORA group leader is convinced that, despite the restrictive conditions, such an experiment should be conducted in order to introduce real changes in research evaluation and move towards open science, replication of results, and free sharing of knowledge. Open science (scientific research and results to be made available to all inquisitive people, amateurs and professionals) is one of the priorities of the European Commission, and it has been formally introduced in numerous Community documents (European Commission, Directorate-General for Research and Innovation, 2020, 2018). Open science contributed to changes in the business models of

---

3 Get Involved Awards 2022 – University of Plymouth (last visited April 29, 2022).

publishing and accessing the academic research. It democratised the access to the research along with the flourishing of social repositories of academic research such as researchgate.net and academia.edu. Available funding from the European Union programmes increased availability of research to wider audiences (including the start-up community). At the same time predatory publishers applied a complex of marketing techniques to increase citations of the papers published in their open access outlets and to get around the quality controls of the major scientific databases. Various authors doubt the promise of the open science (Böschen et al, 2020) and especially its expected impact on policy making.

Over the last few years, common principles have been commented on and imposed with the aim of resolving part of the existing issues. These principles are not binding, but they correspond to the desire to implement a more independent, transparent, and clear evaluation of research outcome. This trend is observed in the more frequent citation of documents, such as the Leiden Manifesto (2015). It consists of ten principles which are grouped around pre-defined evaluation indicators, taking into consideration the specificities in different fields, using quantitative indicators in support of quality assessment, and timely updating indicators which no longer adequately correspond to the needs for research evaluation.

The efforts towards more effective research assessment are complemented by the Hong Kong principles, which were formulated and endorsed at the 6th World Conference on Research Integrity in 2019 in Hong Kong. They are formulated as follows (World Conferences on Research Integrity, 2019):

- assess responsible research practices (these would include ethical behaviour);
- value added reporting;
- reward the practice of open science (this is particularly important for the access to knowledge by the global south researchers and shortening the time from publication to implementation in business or society);
- acknowledge the broad range of research activities;
- recognise essential other tasks like peer review and mentoring.

As an important step in the same direction, in November 2021 the European Commission announced intentions to outline a framework for research assessment to be applied by all member countries. The focus is put on rewarding ethics, integrity, teamwork, and diversity of outputs in addition to quality and impact (Nature, 2022).

I. Research Evaluation: What, Why, Who?

Organisations are also established with the goal to support responsible evaluation. Such example is INORMS, Research Evaluation Working Group founded in 2001 (https://inorms.net/research-evaluation-group/). Its goal is to encourage interactions between members and sharing of good practices.

3. Research evaluation: tasks

Research evaluation is not, and should not be, an end in itself – it is rather a component of the decision-making process governing research at different levels. There are four broad reasons to conduct a research evaluation:

- to increase the accountability of researchers, policymakers, and funding bodies in the eyes of society by making the research team present its outputs and impacts;
- to steer the research process towards studying the outcomes;
- to provide means for advocacy to conduct research or to fund it, based on past outcomes;
- to achieve a better understanding and apply the 'lessons learnt' practice from previous attempts for a research process (Georghiou & Larédo, 2005).

In addition, specific steps are needed to close the gap between the lack of the necessary substantive knowledge and the decision-making process. There are five 'insufficient' or incomplete knowledge categories (gaps) which have a direct impact on the decision-making process:

- difficulties in identifying and interpreting facts (a facts gap);
- difficulties in understanding and grasping certain processes which have a cause-effect relation or create conditions for a series of consequences (natural mechanisms gap);
- difficulties in identifying possible indirect effects (systematic gap);
- difficulties and insecurity with regards to introducing a research product in real manufacturing (technological gap);
- lack of interest which could influence subsequent positive actions (strategic elements gap).

Taking this incomplete knowledge into consideration is a key challenge facing research evaluation. The research evaluation process is characterised by guaranteed quality control on execution; it is conducted by independent experts, research committees, or panels, and it offers a compulsory conclusion and recommendations to the relevant political or financial decision-makers – ministry, heads of executive agencies, donors, etc. This can be treated as a process-oriented evaluation practice.

However, in the last decade evaluation practices (especially those related to large European projects and programmes) are much more oriented towards results – private and public. The evaluation can also be defined as a way of identifying the effect (impact) of particular public activities: scientific and technological, public, and, in some cases, political. This activity can be transposed to a past or future period, and it can be direct and indirect.

The conditions for conducting a research evaluation require two types of process relationships: entry/exit (resources and products) and cause/effect (factors and results).

Research evaluation could be conducted on different levels:

- evaluation of proposals for research projects in terms of quality;
- evaluation of completed national and/or international projects and programme activities;
- evaluation of the research conducted by a given academic unit;
- evaluation of the overall national research system.

All of these conditions presume a focus on the quality of the research activity. The following elements can be subject to evaluation:

- an economic and/or social effect which comes as a result from the implementation of one or more research programmes, targeted or joint;
- outcomes and effects generated as a result of the implementation of a given research project/programme;
- research methods and their implementation;
- the research and/or technological level (degree of originality) of a given development.

An independent review of the role of metrics in research evaluation and management in the United Kingdom offers a framework for responsible metrics and a set of recommendations (Wilsdon et al., 2015). The study looks at research evaluation indicators in different disciplines and tries to evaluate the negative or unintended effects of metrics on various aspects of research culture.

I. Research Evaluation: What, Why, Who?

Evaluation indicators can be quantitative and qualitative and can be applied jointly or independently. The figure shows the specificities of the applicable quantitative and qualitative criteria.

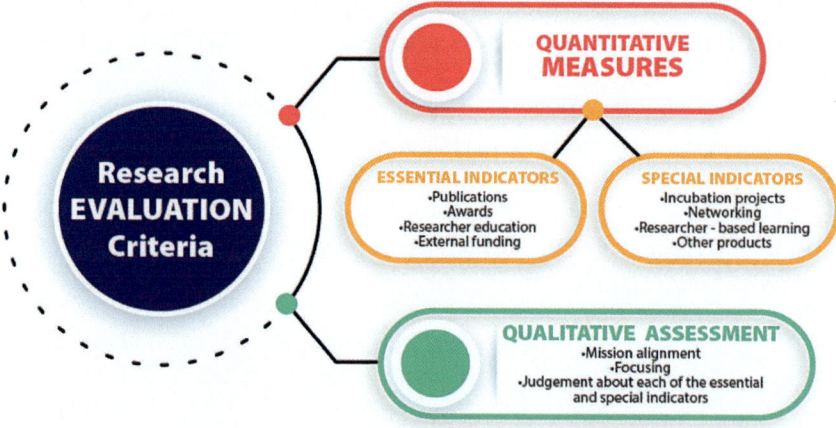

Source: Adapted from Cantu, Bustani, Molina & Moreira (2009).

Figure 1.3: Research Evaluation Criteria

Research evaluation, when properly conducted, improves governance, increases transparency of public funding of higher education and science, contributes to evidence-based decision making with up-to-date information about the quality and impact of the scientific research. Regular and independent research evaluation strengthens the capacity of institutions to conduct strategic planning of their research and in turn increase their competitiveness.

The recommendations of the independent review and analysis of the role of metrics in research evaluation and management in the United Kingdom (Wilsdon et al., 2015) focus on its significance for supporting the effective management of research and on the availability of useful and reliable sources of information to be used in the evaluation process for the purpose of ensuring transparency, avoiding mistakes, carefully using quantitative indicators on the premise that all measures are applied in a coordinated manner. The summarised recommendations from this report (applicable to all research evaluation systems) include:

- Choice and application of indicators — they have to be comprehensible for the research community.
- Use of online platforms and tools which can improve access and visibility of scientific research, as well as opportunities for data sharing.
- Expert evaluation of particular activities which, despite some shortcomings and limitations, continues to receive broad support in different disciplines.
- Application of qualitative and quantitative indicators which correspond to individual disciplines and context. (The 'one size fits all' approach is less likely to work in all cases. The unsuitable indicators distort the motivation of a given researcher and the vision for his/her research.)
- Open, transparent and clear structure for research data. There is a growing tendency of journals to request full data-sharing of published papers.
- Complying with common data description, data collection and data disclosure standards.

The evaluation has to be conducted in a way that 'excess' effects are eliminated. For example, when using a lot of frequent evaluation procedures, new initiatives might be destroyed, and a lot of resources could be taken away from the creative process.

Based on studies of numerous research evaluation initiatives and analyses, research evaluation could be understood **as a complex social practice managed by funding agencies or ministries** (Elzinga, 1995). That practice could be subdivided into several elements:

- Social process, ensuring legitimation of policy-making or administrative decision-making, as well as raising transparency of state funds spending on research.
- Setting up expectations, providing a basis for an adequate and effective use of the funds granted (the socio-economic effect is usually applied as a metric – the result of the development).
- Precise steering and correction of workplans and programmes on institutional level as a result of feedback from evaluation results, similar to the peer-review on a paper-level.
- Achieving a rich information infrastructure which could be useful in the decision-making process.

Different 'schools' studying the research evaluation have different specificities, but at the end of the day they show some common characteristics:

- Increasing rationality in evaluation where the focus moves from 'formalising a past activity' to 'improving the understanding about the course of action in the future' and setting the focus on 'strategic research' as opposed to 'curiosity research'. This is especially valid in countries where national foresight projects exist. In case the private sector also applies the scenario planning techniques, the research priorities derived from the back-casting contribute to the strategic research agenda.
- Expanding the coverage of the evaluation from 'a problem-specific one' to a 'broader one' or 'systemic one', involving analysis of stakeholders' relationships.
- Expanding the number of stakeholders, who, along with an 'objective external evaluation', offer their own analysis or evaluation.

We could conceptualise all these characteristics of the systemic approach within the context of complex social practice (Elzinga, 1995) as a holistic approach. The holistic approach would see research evaluation in all layers or contexts of social practice – managerial, economic, social, and environmental sustainability. Organisational (including managerial) readiness to foresee trends in science or social, economic, and environmental shocks and its capacity to respond to those shocks should be included as an issue of assessment. The holistic approach requires widening the range of the consulted stakeholders in all phases – from policy formulation to evaluation of results. They should include the users of research results but also the society as a whole – civil society organisations and local unorganised communities. Science communication is also an integral part of the mandate of research organisations. Although researchers typically are not ready to engage in social marketing of their research, it is part of their social responsibility to outreach to the society – be it children at school, who might become the next researchers, or civil society organisations, policy makers, and businesses.

4. Types of research evaluation

The types of research evaluation are, to a large extent, linked to the expectations about its nature, the way it is performed, the tasks carried out, and the manner of addressing the relevant group of stakeholders.

Some authors categorise research evaluation based on the applicable approaches (Worthen et al., 1997):

- Objectives-oriented – focuses on determining the objectives and the degree to which they have been achieved.
- Management-oriented – focuses on determining the information which managers/decision-makers need.
- Consumer-oriented – focuses on providing information to the consumer and on the evaluation of different competing 'products' and services. Consumers here refer to public institutions interested in the new policy design, businesses which need relevant research-intensive product/service, and socially responsible investors, which are accountable to society.
- Expert-oriented – built on the basis of particular experts who determine the quality of the topic which is being evaluated.
- Consultation-oriented and process-oriented – brings together different points of view of the evaluators and compares the pros and cons.
- Participation-oriented – takes into account the variety of viewpoints presented, the values, the criteria, and the needs defined by the stakeholders.

Rossi and Freeman (1999) present the classification of the stakeholder groups which are directly involved or interested in the evaluation process of a given research programme:

- Politicians and decision makers – responsible for deciding the future actions in relation to the programme which is being evaluated.
- Programme sponsors – responsible for financing the evaluation.
- Target participants – entities or units that are at the receiving end of the service being evaluated.
- Programme management – a group which is responsible for the programme.
- Programme staff – a group which delivers the programme.
- Evaluators – a group which conducts the evaluation.
- Programme competitors – groups which compete with the programme.
- Contextual stakeholders – groups in the encirclement of the programme.
- Evaluating community – independent (or second round) evaluators who determine the quality of the evaluation.

Even though individual groups of stakeholders have different influence and perceive the evaluation results in a different way, the stakeholders' expectations become part of the process.

A wide segment of research assessments is focused on outcomes or results, which are of interest to different target groups. Due to quantitative nature of outcome-oriented evaluations, it creates an illusion for higher objectivity and through quantitative indicators policymakers believe it is easier to prove a given statement. Because of criticism towards the more quantitative approach the system adopts more and more quantifiable proxies. It is quite rarely to find qualitative indicators with a central place in the evaluation system.

Therefore, the outcome-based criteria system is increasingly detailed, and the process evaluation system is not monitored, analysed, and developed. Moreover, it becomes more and more bureaucratised and acquires purely administrative functions. Embedding innovative experimental forms of assessment based on quality will certainly change the general picture of the assessment process and the system will become more flexible, losing some of its rigidity.

According to the European Commission, Directorate-General for Research and Innovation (1997), the evaluation has to be:

- analytical – to apply accepted methodologies for qualitative and quantitative analyses but also participative practices ensuring different viewpoints;
- systematic – to follow a carefully prepared strategy with detailed planning and consistently implemented at different level of system;
- reliable: To evaluate the same data, the application of the same mechanisms must lead to the same results regardless of who the evaluator is. Although subjectivity is inevitable, it should be processed in such way that the result of the evaluation is independent of the participating evaluators, provided they meet certain academic performance criteria.

4. Types of research evaluation

Source: Adapted from Hong & Boden (2003).

Figure 1.4: Architecture of the programme evaluation system

Although the EC defines three main characteristics of research assessment, and all of them include a process evaluation element, very few assessment systems contain objective criteria for processes evaluation.

The main time-related types of evaluations are *ex ante* – an initial evaluation prior to the implementation of the programme or before the decision for project funding. This is the most frequently used evaluation type. Other types are:

- Mid-term – mid-term evaluation: This could involve ongoing monitoring and feedback which is provided based on the results obtained during the implementation of the project/programme activities. It is an insepar-

able part of the evaluation procedure because it provides effective control during the whole project/programme cycle in view of minimising the risk in their implementation.
- *Ex-post* evaluation – being applicated after the completion of a given programme/project (*ex-post* evaluations are rarely and not systematically used. Sometimes they are overdue and implemented only formally). Sometimes *ex-post* evaluations include impact assessments.

In relative terms, the *ex-ante* evaluation is the most clearly defined procedure in the evaluation process. It is widely used in institutions which finance research, as well as in the evaluation of the preliminary plans of research organisations. The criteria used in this type of evaluation are, to a large extent, harmonised, especially on their base level. In specific cases, a second, smaller set of criteria, which reflect the specificity of the particular activity, is included. In general cases the type or impact of the criteria changes, and this is in line with the general balance between applicable criteria.

The mid-term evaluation aims to evaluate the progress in terms of achieving the set goals. It provides an opportunity to make timely changes in order to guarantee that these goals are achieved within the time planned. This type of evaluation provides an opportunity to determine whether:

- the intervention is still aligned with the strategic goals set;
- it is suitable and useful for the key stakeholders;
- it is conducted in an efficient way.

The ex-post evaluation is more difficult to perform, and in a lot of the cases it is conducted as a matter of formality due to the fact that:

- scientific research is not a routine activity with a final limited outcome, thus the quality of the results can be evaluated only at a particular stage;
- scientific research is part of the national innovation ecosystem, and the latter can be evaluated in different aspects;
- only some of the criteria are used in the evaluation – the ones which are applied in the evaluation of the proposals for a given development.

It reports the following types of accompanying activities:

- audit-type evaluation;
- evaluation of policies related to strategic research;

- evaluation of the efficiency of functioning of the entire research system (university, research institute);
- impact.

The ex-post and mid-term evaluations are particularly needed in terms of future development of programmes and activities. In recent years (between 2008 and 2018, depending on the programming period) the impact evaluation of part of the activities under the operational programmes of the Structural Funds has been subject to analysis for the majority of new member states. Impact evaluation, however, is based on formalised and, in some cases, unsuitable criteria, and it can be difficult for it to act as a homologue of the *ex-post* evaluation.

The evaluation system in European programmes and projects, to a large extent, applies harmonised basic criteria, and it has created a common framework for their application. Due to the fact that this type of evaluation assesses only intentions and possible outcomes, the degree of uncertainty is very high, and this type of evaluation is more easily digested both by the evaluator and the person being evaluated.

Some evaluation activities of framework programmes of the Community, the programmes of European structures (for example JRC, ECA), can be referred to the last type of evaluation. This evaluation applies the assessment of some typical performance indicators and takes into consideration as well proven effectiveness for the economy or/and society as a result of programme realisation. It is used as an input to outline the framework of programme development in the future.

The types of evaluations, organisation method and relevant activities are systematised in Table 1.1.

Table 1.1: Types of evaluation

Types of evaluation activities	Subjects of evaluation			Expected impact
	Research projects with a clearly defined outcome	**Grants for strategic research programmes**	**Projects and technological and innovation activity**	
	Activities for conducting the evaluation process according to subject groups			
Ex ante	A system of evaluators who evaluate the proposals offered, based on a set of criteria	A system of evaluators and consumers evaluating the research quality and the expected economic and public benefits, based on a set of criteria. The expectations of state structures and consumers also impact the evaluation.	A system of experts, including consumers and sponsors/donors who are organised in ad-hoc groups. Addressing the expectations of a given consumer group is of key importance	Ensuring legitimisation and transparency of the public finances provided. A basis for effective use of the funds provided.
Mid term	A system of evaluators who evaluate the progress of the mid-term results, based on a set of criteria.	A system of evaluators, consumers and public structures evaluating the progress in the implementation of a given programme, the quality, and the expected economic and public benefits.	A system of experts, including consumers and sponsors/donors who evaluate the progress and the impact which is the result of the implementation of a given stage of the technological and innovation activity.	Careful monitoring and correction of work plans and programmes as a result of feedback from evaluation results.
Ex post	A system of evaluators who provide a conclusion by comparing the expected results which were originally evaluated and the results achieved in reality	A panel of experts evaluating the degree of achievement with regards to the strategic goals.	A panel of experts and professional evaluators who evaluate the results achieved, based on a comparison with the set expectations from the implementation of a given project.	Achieving a rich information infrastructure.

Source: Authors' own elaboration.

Depending on the subject of evaluation, the evaluation objectives can be very different. We can differentiate the following types of evaluation activities:

- Evaluation of a given research structure – a research institute or a small company with a research profile. This type of activity is performed vis-

ibly or away from the public eye; it develops individually and has clearly defined cause-effect relations. The reason for its implementation is because the activity of such units does not just need 'public recognition' but also accountability before the society, in addition to arguments for future financing.
- An evaluation of the general research and technological development is more frequently implemented with the help of international organisations and experts and clearly impacts future policy-related decisions and the introduction of policies, reforms, new structures and programmes promoted on a national level.
- A programme-based evaluation – the most recent evaluation introduced – is aimed at institutionalisation, defining the degree of applicability and usability of the outcome achieved and the effectiveness of its implementation.

The effects of research and technological activity, which can be evaluated, are systematised in Table 1.2.

Table 1.2: Effects from research and technological activity which are subject to evaluation

Main groups of activities financed by the public budget	Direct effect		Indirect effect	
	Short-term	Long-term	Short-term	Long-term
Science	Specific scientific knowledge	Cognitive knowledge	Improved training / research training	Economic/ public benefits
Economy and society	Improved technologies and social cohesion	Better know-how Balanced social relationships	Improved and environmentally friendly productivity Social consensus	Better competitiveness Prosperous society
Policies	Better understanding and implementation of new policies	Resolving social/economic issues	Grasping the genesis of existing issues	Contributing toward reaching a consensus when resolving existing issues

Source: Authors' own elaboration.

Evaluation methods can be examined using a matrix structure in which the elements of the matrix are the data, the type of evaluation, and the analysis applied. The data can be quantitative (statistical and bibliometric) and qualitative – gathered through interviews, statements by focus groups, surveys, etc. The analysis can be different – conducted through peer review panels, based on different studies, technological evaluation, etc.

The indicators used are varied, but a small part of them are basic and are used in almost all types of research evaluations. These are illustrated in Table 1.3.

Table1.3: Types of indicators

Indicators	Quantity	Quality
Entry	Research staff State of the art of the subject of evaluation	Strategically planned research activities, impact of knowledge absorption
During the activity	Citability of research publications Patents, utility models *Note: Measurable in terms of quantity (number)*	Where the publication is published (presence of an impact factor) What is the type of the patent
Exit	Increased productivity, new workplaces, additional profit, value added Social conflict/issue resolved	Completely new and environmentally friendly products, services, processes Opening new markets and/or market niches, expanding an existing market Entering a global market

Source: Authors' own elaboration.

The first two types of indicators are linked to the research process, while the last type, the exit indicators, are oriented towards finding specific and socio-economic results.

It should be taken into account the fact that, in some cases, evaluation may lead to limitations in the research and technological activity, but at the same time it is still aimed at comprehensive coverage. The comprehensive coverage and the effects of the evaluation activity are illustrated on the diagram of Figure 1.5.

4. Types of research evaluation

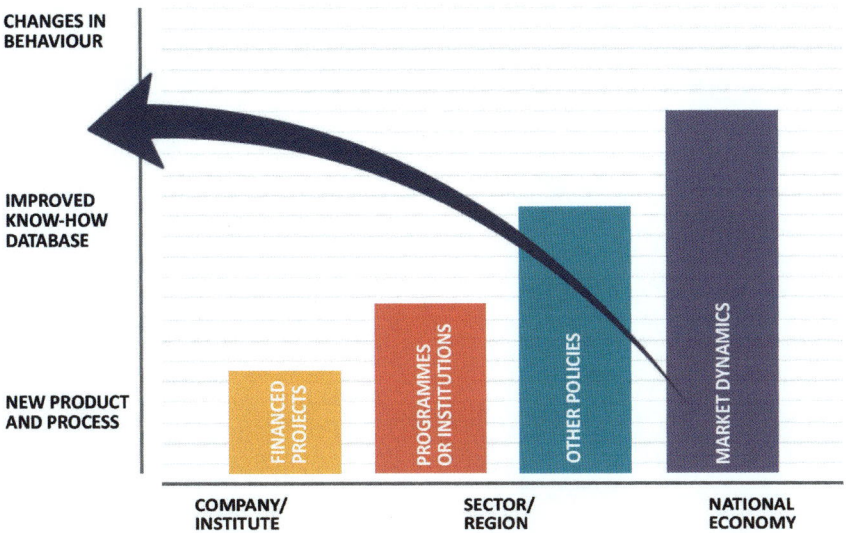

Source: Adapted from Accreditation Agency, the Netherlands.

Figure 1.5: Diagram of the effect of technological activity

Figure 1.6 illustrates the five-steps model of the institutional research evaluation framework.

Source: Adapted from Hassanain, Anil & Abdo (2016).

Figure 1.6: Framework concept for institutional research evaluation

If the research in a given region is being evaluated, the most frequently used applicable indicators are as follows:

- gross government expenditures for research as a share of the gross domestic product;

- research expenditures provided by the business relative to public expenses;
- workforce employed in the research sector (this includes research organisations and research institutes);
- research expenditures per capita from the working population or per researcher.

The following entry indicators are used for institutional or individual research activity:

- total number of publications in peer-reviewed and indexed journals for which the previous evaluation period is completed;
- total number of citations;
- patents, utility models or technology transferred products in the economy;
- number of PhD candidates who have successfully defended their thesis, for a given period, which is most often determined by using the evaluation methodology.

The following exit indicators for evaluating institutional or personal research are also observed:

- number of publications for the evaluation period in peer-reviewed journals (3–5 years);
- exchange of researchers between research organisations/universities or between research organisations and companies;
- participation/funds attracted under different European programmes;
- participation/funds attracted under national programmes and industry contracts;
- memberships in international research organisations;
- memberships in editorial teams of scientific journals;
- research awards (international and national), etc.

5. Evaluation procedures based on scientometrics

Some authors use mathematical tools for the purpose of creating a model for the growth trend in publications and suggest the term 'scientometrics' for this kind of research (De Bellis, 2009). Scientometrics can be defined as a "quantitative study of science, communication in science and science policy" (Hess, 1997). It has been developing over time. It studies indices for improving the extraction of information from peer-reviewed research publications (usually described as a 'bibliometric' analysis of science) and has gradually expanded to other types of documents and sources of information related to science and technologies.

The scientometric indicators complement and contribute for the standardisation, collection, and analysis of a wide range of activities in the field of science, technologies, and innovation by providing evidence for a selected set of results in science and technologies. There are certain advantages to quantitative approaches in evaluation, using proper statistical data and suitable indicators.

Weinberg (1989) claims that the Board on Physics of the US National Academy of Sciences has applied evaluations to three types of criteria: internal, external, and structural. These have been divided because the inherent indicators include the significance of the research topic, the potential for discovering fundamental laws, the potential for discovering summaries which could be broadly applied, and the attractiveness and maturity of the research. External measures review the potential contribution and stimulation for other sciences, in particular engineering, medicine, and applied sciences, and the contribution towards the national prestige, defence, public education, and international cooperation. The last set of criteria evaluates the need for progress in the discipline and the need to maintain the development in a specific field.

6. Bibliometric indicators

Bibliometric indicators provide answers to the following questions:

- How productive is a given research team or an individual researcher (or what is the essence of their/his/her research), what is their level of research competence on an international level?
- Where is the team or the individual researcher positioned in comparison to similar teams in the country and abroad (benchmarking)?

The main limitations to bibliometrics are results which are predominantly applicable to research groups, units and institutions, and which are difficult to apply to innovation activities which have a bigger coverage and do not focus specifically on pure research results. Nevertheless, the increasing capacity of scientific results imputedly intervenes the competitive innovation process via growing intellectual capacity, proved by improved bibliometric indicators (Vutsova, 2009).

According to Leiden's Manifesto (Hicks et al., 2015) with regards to monitoring the citability of publications, there are often comments about the increasing reliance on concrete data from large databases, namely Web of Science, which has an impact factor that dominates as an indicator in a lot of research evaluation models. Meanwhile, it is not entirely universal. For example, a group of European historians receive a relatively low evaluation because they publish books, not articles in peer-reviewed journals (Hicks & Wouters, 2015). This issue could be avoided by carefully clarifying the specifics in different fields and adding normalising correctives.

Another element which may not be taken into consideration in the impact-factor-based research evaluation is the regional importance of the research despite the fact that Web of Science is undertaking corrective actions in this respect (it includes more journals of regional importance, which are visible in the main data collection, or creates specialised national databases similar to the ones in Norway and Croatia). On the other hand, this is one of the platforms where the biggest amount of information is exchanged in the field of science, and hence access to results is guaranteed.

Problematic fields are mainly those of social sciences and humanities, especially when national/regional issues are examined which would not be of such big interest to international journals. Even in cases a significant global impact has been achieved, as in the case of organisation of the International Philosophy Olympiad (Kolev, 2017), most of the researchers behind it never publish in WoS/Scopus. A balance must be achieved between regional journals included in large databases and monitoring the quality of those which are not. Very often, the evaluation is based on the percentile in which the publication is included.

In the evaluation of research projects, for example, a taxonomic tree of the criteria can be used in view of determining their significance.

6. Bibliometric indicators

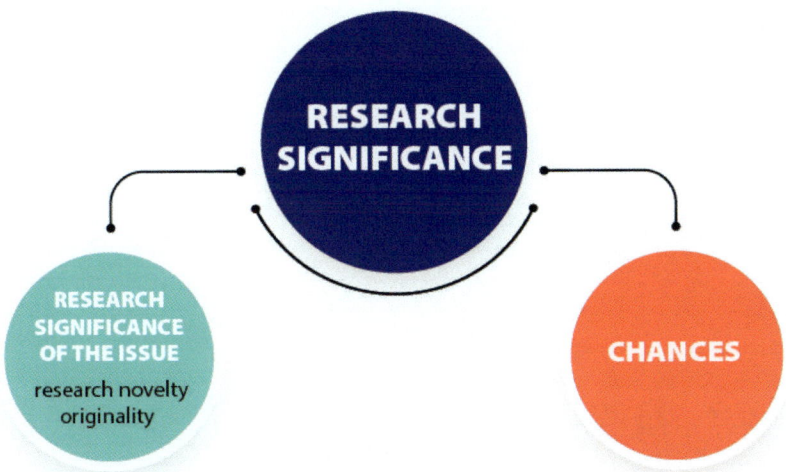

Source: Adapted from German Recotrs' Conference.

Figure 1.7: Taxonomy of scientific research

Scientometrics mainly relies on clearly structured situations which determine the reliability and applicability of its methods. It uses statistical data processing which in some cases creates complications in the analysis. Inaccurate or incorrect conclusions may sometimes be drawn, which significantly differ from the evaluators' opinion.

I. Research Evaluation: What, Why, Who?

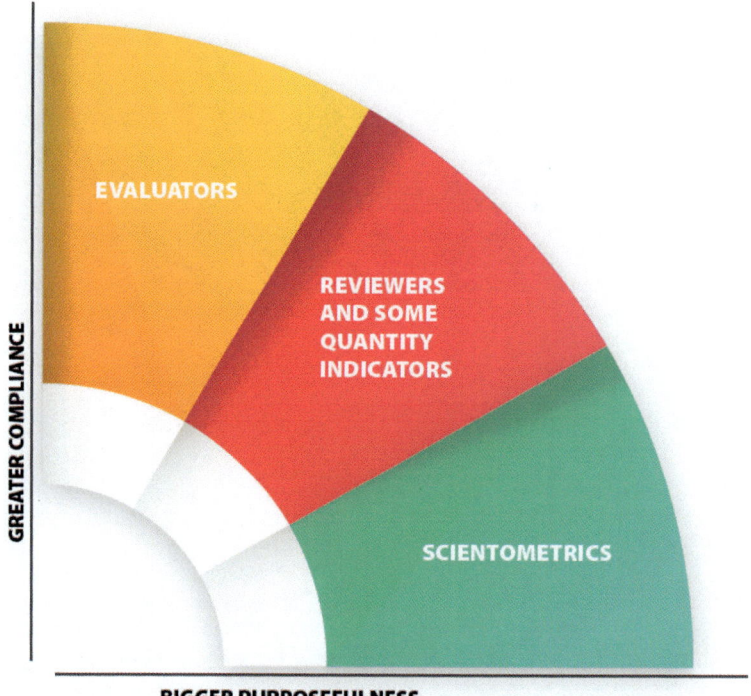

Source: Adapted from Accreditation Agency, the Netherlands.

Figure 1.8: Evaluation methods

Statistical problems which might occur are related to ranking, might be the result of the discrete nature of citation distributions, especially with small samples, and applied a fractional solution (Waltman et al., 2012). In response to such potential threats Bornmann and Williams (2020) suggest guidelines and procedures for the normalisation of percentile ranks based on cumulative frequencies in percentages. University ranking systems are also targeted because of the methodology of assessing research outputs (Fauzi et al., 2018; Bowden, 2000). To tackle these challenges, some authors (Szomszor et al., 2021) believe that new indicators are not necessary, but efforts should be directed towards choosing (a combination of) the proper ones in order to present academic research more adequately. For better decision making a focus on the management and interpretation of results should be put.

In the evaluation of industrial and applied research the main goal is to determine the contribution towards achieving the company's strategy and objectives. In order to support a given industrial research, the following entry indicators for evaluation should be adhered to:

- the expected effects of the research;
- integrating them with the business strategy of the company;
- the available portfolio of intellectual products;
- monitoring process;
- possible losses due to poor execution compared to the achievements expected.

Apart from that, the results and/or the environment in which industrial research is going to be developed and/or applied are also evaluated through:

- percentage of the turnover generated from innovative products[4];
- percentage of the real innovative products on the market – maintaining a sustainable market;
- the degree of technological innovation of the company;
- granted patents as well as a ratio of the granted patent/applications;
- revenue from the provision of IPR products;
- variety of the technological structure – spin-off, spill over, incubation units, etc.;
- staff involved in R&D activities.

Measuring the effect of industrial research is usually difficult. The Office of Technology Assessment (1986) in the US presents three main reasons in support of their argument as to why measuring the effect of RTD is difficult. Firstly, there are non-economic goals, especially in relation to public and socially desired high-risk investments, such as defence, for example. There is uncertainty in their measurement, for example, progress in healthcare.

In addition, the evaluation criteria are highly contextualised to the national innovation system. In countries where the stock-markets are relatively underdeveloped the role of patents is less-significant compared to US, for instance. Smaller firms in countries with weak law enforcement tend to protect their innovations through classical commercial secrecy.

---

4 3M for instance applies milestone indicators for a share of revenue generated by new products which are the result of internal research, development, and innovation activities.

Third, well-known shortcoming of indicators for industrial research is the lack of a transparent ex-post evaluation. One of the reasons for this is also the existence of another regime of company research which takes the competitive conditions on the market into account. Often in relation with this, such researchers are not allowed to publish and disseminate results. At the same time many companies use co-publications with academics as a marketing and legitimisation strategy.

There is another type of evaluation criteria – time-bound relevant indicators. They cover measurable values related to a specific period of time.

If a specific programme is being evaluated (for instance, Cosmic Research), the applicable indicators have to be appropriately selected in order to ensure adequate measurable values. In a lot of cases the indicators are comparable, which allows using an average indicator – for example an average number of citations of one publication by one researcher. In addition, evaluation can be provided for science education and indicators for research management.

In some cases, when the evaluation process covers more than one activity, the different indicators are showcased by presenting all factors influencing the evaluation process. That is how the 'information processing' model is created. The model comprises a set of seven stakeholder target groups or/and interesting parties intervened by the evaluation. This approach is illustrated through the so-called 'radar diagram' (Figure 1.9).

6. Bibliometric indicators

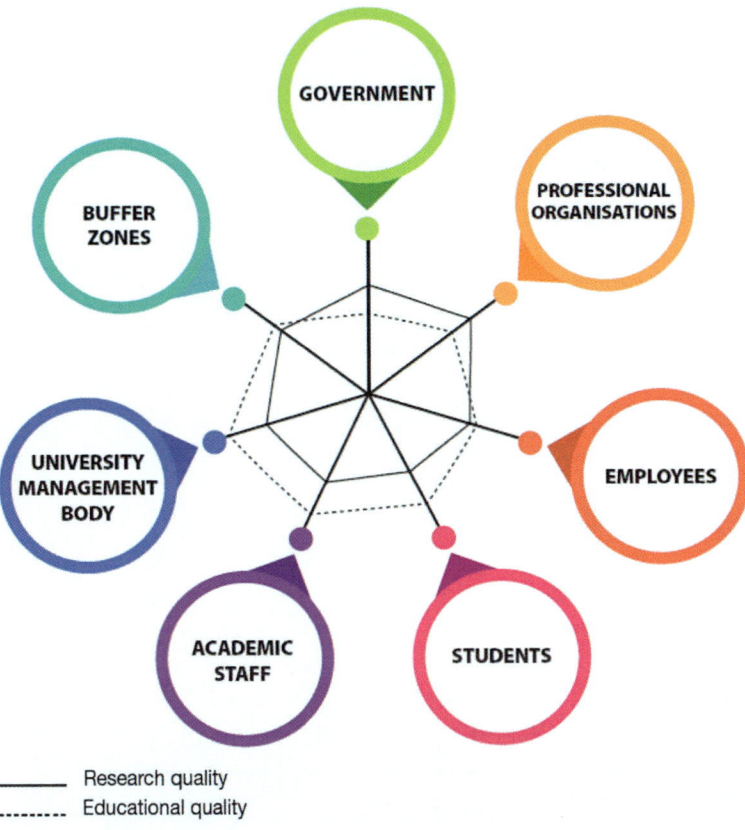

———— Research quality
·········· Educational quality

Source: Adapted from Accreditation Agency, the Netherlands.

Figure 1.9: Radar diagram

The indicators which are applied to the management evaluation adhere to a time schedule and address the interests of stakeholders.

The general applicable evaluation methods deal with entry results, exit results, and results from the point of view of the consumers – assessed universities and society. Evaluation methods vary, as is shown below.

6.1. Evaluation procedures based on expert conclusions

These methods are based on the reviewers' work at the entrance and exit and are focused on:

- evaluating the expectations and, consequently, the research output from the point of view of a research achievement;
- evaluating the result from the point of view of the consumer.

The evaluation conducted by reviewers is most commonly used. It is rooted in tradition and is accepted by the academic body. However, it should be taken into account that there may be deviations due to the lack of balance in the selection of reviewers, resulting in poorly evaluated multidisciplinary studies regardless of the fact that the results are the best exit indicator. That is why this type of expertise is best applied in research-oriented developments. It is accompanied by compulsory collection of adequate data and selection of reviewers.

In the evaluation of specific results through consumers, the issue is made more complicated due to the fact that the latter are directly affected by the execution of a given project and cannot be independent because they know the team that develops the product, and in some cases the final effect impacts more than one project or programme. The effectiveness of integrating a given result, the synergy effect, if there is one, and the extent to which the result obtained is suitable for the intervened system also have an impact in this respect.

6.2. Socio-economic models for research evaluation

In this model, apart from the traditional scientometric indicators, other methods are used as well – surveys, investigative visits, micro and macroeconomic analyses, comparative analyses, studies of best practices, etc. Nevertheless, an adequate balance between the significance of each one of them has to be sought.

Each of the methods used takes into consideration the objectives of the intentions set in the programme (project) and the development of the programme model, and it applies a realistic approach with regards to the objectives and the designated tasks. For example, the evaluation questions of interim evaluation of Horizon 2020 programme focus exactly on the relevance of the programme, whether it developed as it was expected and if it was adaptive and effective. It includes not only monitoring reports and extensive analysis of the programme itself but also external horizontal studies, data from different EU institutions, input from various stakeholders, and surveys (Interim evaluation of Horizon 2020).

The dynamic of the evaluative process as a series of consecutive actions and in terms of time span is illustrated in Figure 1.10.

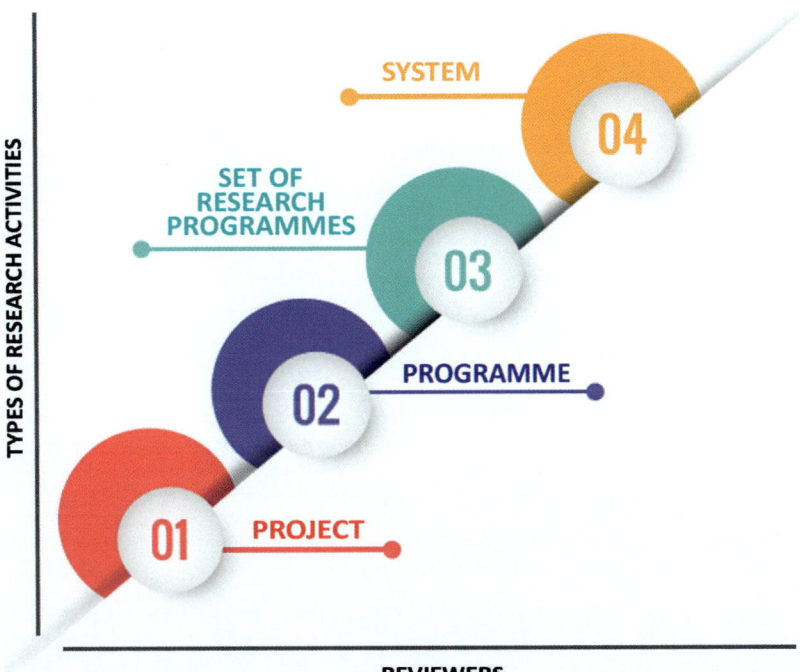

Source: Adapted from Accreditation Agency, the Netherlands.

Figure 1.10: Dynamic of the evaluative process

The peer review evaluation system is practically applied to each of the above-mentioned modules which are subject to evaluation. Figure 1.11. illustrates a full evaluation cycle and includes the following elements:

I. Research Evaluation: What, Why, Who?

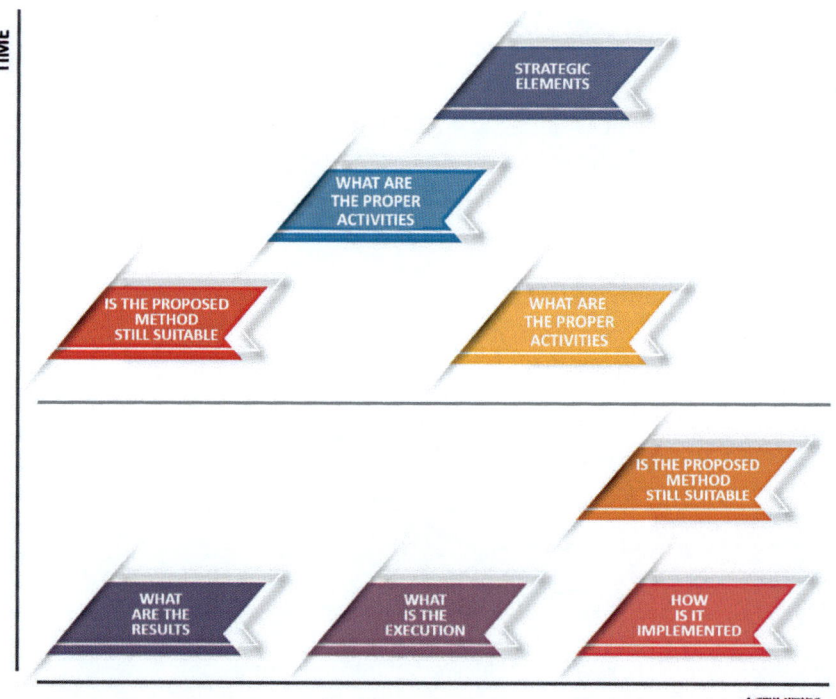

Source: Adapted from Accreditation Agency, the Netherlands.

Figure 1.11: Levels of activities, subject to evaluation

The specificity of the evaluation process implies the presence of several groups of criteria, for example: to evaluate research projects applying for financing; to evaluate results from completed projects; for institutional evaluation. Each group of criteria contains a specific set of metrics. The majority of them are standardised for different evaluation practices.

6.3. New research evaluation methods

Over time, evaluation methods have evolved by adding new sets of criteria and/or shifting the focus of relevance. The new trends have the ambition to achieve a more complex and truthful assessment. New elements are introduced in the evaluation practice.

The need to evaluate the social impact of science and the aim to achieve a more complete evaluation of research have led to the creation of alternative indicators and approaches. One approach, SCOPE, is suggested by the INORMS Research Evaluation Group. The abbreviation means:

- Start with what you value;
- Context considerations;
- Options for evaluating;
- Probe deeply;
- Evaluate your evaluation.

The supporters of the approach advise first determining the aim of the evaluation and the risks associated to it. The different types of evaluation may affect differently the evaluated, whether we are looking at individuals, institutions, or at national level. Both quantitative and qualitative measures have their imperfections and have to be applied with caution. Still, steps could be taken to mitigate possible negative effects. As for quantitative indicators, they could be used in combination as a 'basket of indicators' and along with qualitative assessment. Among the latter, peer review could be improved through using appropriate experts, more than one and diverse reviewers, and again together with using metrics where appropriate.

An important aspect of the SCOPE model is that the assessment should be conducted in concert with the evaluated individuals or teams. In this way, the evaluator would better understand their aims and the joint interpretation of results would lead to openness and transparency.

Sometimes the evaluation process might have unintended consequences both at institutional and individual levels. Some examples are neglecting activities which aren't measured, discouraging initiative, focusing on the short term, or the academic burden when some academics leave the profession or narrow their publications according to the assessment criteria. That is why it is essential to review or evaluate the evaluation. In this way responsible parties could stay open to adjustments and make sure that the methods they are using are effective (INORMS, 2020).

The aim of some of the additional indicators is to provide additional information which bibliometric indicators cannot. Examples of such evidence regarding research effectiveness are, for example, the number of downloads of a given article or the views and references in social media.

One of the most popular additions to bibliometric indicators is altmetrics. Altmetrics uses indicators for research evaluation based on the activity in online tools and environments (Priem, 2014). Altmetrics.org and Altmetric.com are websites which encourage the use of altmetrics. Altmetric.com aims to popularise and disseminate its products in relation to big academic publishing institutions and financing entities (for example, Taylor & Francis, Wiley, The London School of Economics, and Smithsonian).

In terms of measuring tools, altmetrics are classified based on the function which they offer and the type of users who are interested in the given research outcome. For example, these are categories of different types of altmetrics according to their main functions: discussions, references, readers, reviews, videos and citations.

An evaluation of an article is made by calculating how often it is mentioned in different media platforms, i.e., the popularity of the article is based on how often it is referenced in these sources. In addition to the frequency of referencing, altmetrics uses other measures for viewing, disseminating, and impact indicators.

Even though altmetrics cannot be an alternative to traditional bibliometric indicators, it complements them. The advantage is in the speed in which it gathers and reflects information, something that cannot be said about the other, more frequently used research evaluation indicators. The main limitations to this approach are as follows:

- In case of malicious use of the system, unrealistic results may be generated based on the desire of a specific consumer.
- There is no clear correlation between altmetrics and bibliometrics. The former one includes information from social media such as Facebook and Twitter, which are not academic communities; thus, there is a significant risk that the fundamental research may be neglected.
- The sources of information are not exhaustive.
- There is lack of clarity in the definition and interpretation of a given concept.

Despite these factors, altmetrics is perceived as an area of interest and future research.

Two authors (Herrmannova & Knoth, 2016) have introduced the concept of semanometrics as a new group of research evaluation indicators. They are based on the prerequisite that in order to evaluate a given publication, the full text is needed. The authors believe that a new metric for measuring the impact, which takes the full text of the manuscript into consideration, could be developed by reporting the number of citations and views, and the contribution of the manuscript. They believe that semanometrics has the potential to evaluate to a sufficient degree the quality of research and its contribution.

Another group of authors (Lee, West & Howe, 2017) has established a significant link between the scientific impact and the use of visual information. According to them, the bigger the impact of a given research, the more likely it is to include more diagrams, but on the condition that this number varies a lot in individual areas and is applicable only for some sciences. The aim is to study the organisation of visual information because these information-rich objects are largely ignored in bibliometrics and scientometrics research in comparison to citations and text. The authors introduce the concept of visiometrics in order to discover more interesting and useful applications for their idea.

7. Ethics in research evaluation

National research assessment systems are very different, and they have an impact on the research strategies of research departments. Whitley (2007) highlights that research assessment systems affect the organisation and management of knowledge. The robust assessment systems with high standards, rules, and officially established procedures concerning assessment and publishing of results most definitely influence the research strategies of universities and research organisations in a different way depending on the individual research fields. In addition, the connection between policy and assessment may have an impact on the quality of the research. According to Pleger (2016), assessments are performed in a given political context, and they are influenced by it.

Different researchers believe that the study of ethics with regards to performing a research assessment is an underdeveloped field (Gedutis & Biagetti, 2019). There is a lack of shared understanding as to what ethics are, and the standards for quality and competence are regularly confused with the term 'ethics'. It is not clear what the role of ethics is and who is responsible for implementing ethical practices (Williams, 2016).

Biagetti, Gedutis and Ma (2020) represent research evaluation ethics combining aspects from both research and evaluation good practices. The authors claim that there aren't enough clear guidelines how to establish proper criteria and avoid bias and conservatism in peer review.

I. Research Evaluation: What, Why, Who?

Source: Adapted from Biagetti, Gedutis & Ma (2020).

Figure 1.12:   Research Evaluation Ethics between Research Ethics and Evaluation Ethics

A lot of authors (Biagetti et al., 2020) note that a number of issues arise during the assessment process, and those are mainly related to the interpretation of bibliometrics.

It is believed that the results-based indicators have to measure the value of research in an objective manner, but the research community believes that they are often a reason for the occurrence of new forms of manipulation. Since the research assessment relies on approximate (proxy) indicators which only measure indirectly what they should actually present (quality, impact, or social significance), it is increasingly difficult to establish to what extent some or all of the indicators are manipulated and to what extent given high-value studies are authentic. According to some authors, the assessment process is still chaotic and the role of the indicators is not quite clear; for example, despite the fact that the impact factor of journals is the most popular indicator, it is not the only one applied and is not uniform for all assessments (Wouters, 2020). There are, however, some dominant trends in the quality assessments which are relevant to citation practices. There is a risk that research which is not measured by specific indicators may be neglected, which threatens the search for knowledge on the part of the universities (Wouters, 2020). The criticism against scientometrics in Eastern Europe is more frequently expressed by scholars who justify in this way the lack of publications which enter in popular databases. Individual research departments within a given research structure are often against the introduction of elementary requirements to PhD candidates (for example, an article published in a journal indexed by Scopus or Web of Science), arguing that the majority of their members do not have such requirements. This poses a serious obstacle for increasing the quality of research and the international convertibility of research and PhD education.

Some authors take into account the fact that the indicator-based assessment creates pressure for active publishing (Fanelli, 2020), but they also remark that the latter does not lead to unlawful actions and does not hinder researchers' integrity.

The desire of journal editors to receive a higher impact factor leads to another specific effect: an artificial increase in the citations through the coordinated efforts of a 'citation cartel' of journals. Such 'citation cartels' have been observed more and more often over the past years (Kojaku et al., 2021). Different researchers direct their efforts at the creation of algorithms and methods for their reporting (Kojaku et al., 2021; Koley & Mishra, 2019; Perez et al., 2019) or at the exclusion of such journals from international databases.

There is a possibility of manipulation via the participation of researchers in editorial boards at international publishing houses, which are oriented towards increasing the number of publications by a given university and, respectively, increasing the number of co-authors in order to improve these results (Biagioli & Lippman, 2020). Such behaviour distorts the objective picture of bibliometrics.

Another issue arises when the expert assessment and the citation analysis contradict each other. If we only rely on the expert assessment, does this not slow down the development of interdisciplinary studies, because the focus is on established and favoured methodologies? On the other hand, we cannot rely only on quantitative indicators. We cannot directly interpret the number of publications or citations, which is normalised for a given field, as an indicator for quality or impact. The high number of citations can be due to the presence of a unique empiricism, an exceptional research with great impact, or it can be the result of repetition of studies or the efforts of citation cartels. A small number of citations, on the other hand, can be the result of a research which is not that interesting or of innovative ideas that are still not recognised (Wouters, 2020) or published in a journal which has a limited reach. An expert assessment is needed in such case. That is why the objective research assessment requires an incredible balance and a careful approach to the above-mentioned activities. In addition, the assessment is closely linked to a political vision and, respectively, specific methods, and it is an instrument which shows us what kind of society we want to build (Mol, 2002; Thurtle & Mitchell, 2002).

Governments often conduct reforms and make decisions regarding financing based on the global rankings of universities (Rouet, 2022). In this case the effect of the strategies for achieving impact through publications may be distorted and conditions for manipulation may be created (gaming opportunities) (Biagioli & Lippman, 2020). Sarah de Rijcke and Tereza Stöckelová claim that the focus of European research policies on 'international publication impact' as a substitute for quality increases the division between the 'international' north and the limited south (Rijcke & Stöckelová, 2020).

The unscrupulous application of assessment indicators has been discussed many times, including in the San Francisco Declaration on Research Assessment, The Metrics Tide, the Leiden Manifesto, etc. There is still, however, a lack of common approach and application of ethical principles with regards to research assessment in the preparation of an assessment and/or the selection of the criteria, regardless of what the effects of the assessment process are going to be (Dahler-Larsen, 2012). Part of the studies, which focus on ethical issues related to the assessment, are dedicated to the assessors' ethics (Morris, 2008; Schwandt, 2015) and study the ethical dilemmas in their professional conduct. At the moment, professional ethics to a great extent focuses on everyday issues related to the individual participants in the process. Ethical issues are examined in the context of interpersonal relationships where the focus is on the issues which occur as a result of the relations between assessors and the other stakeholders (Schwandt, 2018). As regards the independence of assessments, the pressure exercised by the stakeholders is identified as an important ethical challenge (Pleger, 2016). Morris (2015) admits that collecting information about how assessors react to ethical conflicts is of vital importance, whilst also being a delicate endeavour, bearing in mind the defensive position which some studies in this field may lead to.

There is a possibility of expressing preference with regards to gender, race, language, career stage, and the interdisciplinarity (Helmer, 2017; Lee et al., 2013). There is also a possibility of neglect with regards to the use of innovative procedures and platforms in the assessment process (Bornmann, 2011; Horbach & Halffman, 2019) due to the habit of implementing the routine methods or tools or due to unwillingness to try a new work method.

A socially responsible assessment is one where the rights, dignity, and cultural values of individuals and groups are taken into account. Professional assessors are encouraged to understand and respect the points of view etc. of all stakeholders (Schwandt, 2018). Studies in the field of ethics with regards to assessment should assist assessors, and the latter should use the positive experience of other assessors (Pleger, 2016).

The European Code of Conduct for Research integrity (ALLEA 2017) is a document which postulates the general principles of research ethics, including reliability, honesty, accountability, etc. According to this document, researchers who participate in the assessment process undertake a serious commitment. They have to consider a number of factors such as the presence of a conflict of interests, confidentiality, respecting the rights of authors, etc.

An inseparable part of the integrity of research is the absence of plagiarism, and when it is discovered it should not be neglected, but rather sanctions should be imposed, which would lead to the loss of an academic position. Unfortunately, in Bulgaria the procedure is often suspended without it leading to a direct negative effect for the person responsible for the act of plagiarism. The only exceptions are for people and cases which have become public knowledge (for example politicians), but even that is not guaranteed. A study by Foltynek and Glendinning (2015) shows significant differences among European countries with regards to their understanding of what plagiarism is and to the attitude towards plagiarism, the preparedness how to avoid it, etc.

In a research system where the number of publications is considered an indicator of 'quality' and is a tool used for encouraging career growth and the allocation of grants, 'recycling' a text or self-plagiarism (as a kind of plagiarism) is a way of increasing the results at the expense of other researchers. This raises the question as to what extent the indicators based on results from publications are important assessment criteria for the allocation of work or grants (Horbach & Halffman, 2019). According to some researchers, the solution to the plagiarism issue is to place a focus on quality, not quantity, in the system of criteria (Feenstra, 2021).

According to Helen Simons, plenary lecturer at The Framing Ethics in Impact Evaluation seminar (Barnett & Munslow, 2014), the ethical guidelines or postulates proposed are mainly intentions, and they often relate to the assessment methodology and to the quality of the assessment with regard to a given product rather than focus on whether the research assessment is correct. According to him, and other authors as well, there is a need for ethical norms based on theory, which would guide the assessors' behaviour and choice. Adherence to ethical norms in research assessment is highly dependent on the context of the general level of ethical behaviour in the given country (corruption levels, rule of law, degree of self-regulation in other fields). According to Biagetti and her co-authors Gedutis and Ma (2020), a mixed approach may be applied with regards to resolving the issues of assessment practices.

One of the important questions with regards to the ethics in research assessment relates to its boundaries and the scope of the field. According to Mustajoki and Mustajoki (2017), the identification of ethical issues is achieved in three ways: (a) by identifying the stakeholders (for example, individuals, groups, communities, animals, ecosystems, future generations, etc.), (b) by understanding the rights and responsibilities of the stakeholders, and (c) by defining the options, i.e. searching for a win-win situation or achieving it to the greatest extent possible for the participating stakeholders. Research assessment, be it preliminary or subsequent, concerns important ethical issues. The aim towards a 'common good' in the assessment of a given study means that, in case of a multidisciplinary or interdisciplinary study, each stakeholder involved in the study must be taken into consideration (ESF, 2011).

Some studies show that part of the assessors accept and stand by the claim that ethics do not relate to assessment and that they have never encountered ethical problems in their work (Morris, 2015; Williams, 2016). At the same time, however, it must be taken into account that a well-financed organisation or project can allocate enough financial resources for assessment (especially an interim one or a final internal or external one), while organisations with poor funding do not have this capacity. This would mean that the practice of research assessment is routine in those places where there is funding, not in the places where the assessment is most needed.

Concerning the study, the following four standards, which to a great extent correlate to the ethical principles, must be observed in assessment procedures:

- **Usefulness** – research assessments must address important issues, and the results expected or received must be clear and comprehensible. They should include reasonable recommendations if there is need of such.

- There should be **realism** with regards to the implementation of a given programme and project, strategic measures, policies, etc. in relation to time and finances.
- **Legitimacy** – the assessments should comply with the respective principles and be institutionally accepted and recognised by the academic community.
- **Accuracy** – the information must be gathered, analysed, reported, and interpreted in an accurate and impartial manner.

The National Science Foundation (USA), NSF, postulates the following four principles in the assessment process: goodwill, trust, professionalism, and confidentiality.

Corporate companies invest a lot in compliance and ethics training. According to Andrew Leigh, there are seven principles of ethics training which underlies its success and might be applied into research evaluation as well.

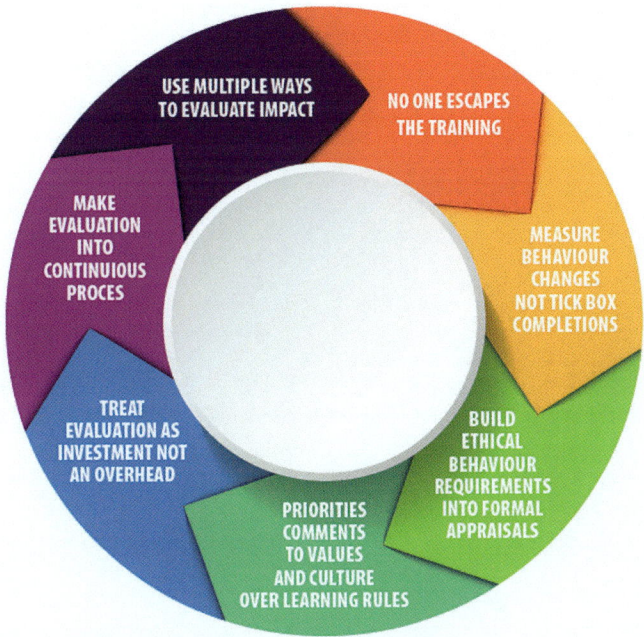

Source: Adapted from Leigh, 2015.

Figure 1.13: *Ethics Evaluation Essentials*

Patton (2014) highlights that studies are something which informs science, while the assessment is something which is targeted at and supports the action itself. In reality, the differentiation between an assessment and a study is rarely that clear, especially with regards to mixed terms about the study of policies, study of the assessment process, or study of the application of results from a given research. The ones in support of the use of experimental methods in the assessment, especially randomised control studies, claim that the knowledge generated is more likely to be precise than approximate, but it is focused on a limited number of issues, and the period for generating it is a lot longer in comparison to the time that is needed to perform applied studies.

Naturally, the assessment process is only one of the factors which contributes to the final result (as studied by Anderson, 2014), but conditions for a distorting effect can be created on all aspects: from the formulation of questions to be the subject of assessment to decisions about the resources, methodologies applied, etc. Adherence to ethical principles supports assessors (and all stakeholders) in their work. Some authors propose a reasonable compromise between the methodological rigor of the assessment process and the assessment itself as a form of knowledge which has to be discussed and used not only by people in positions of power but by the civil society as well. This is quite acceptable when there are a lot of active financial instruments and the specific expectations of each of them are varied.

References

Abramo, G., D'Angelo, C. A., & Grilli, L. (2021). The effects of citation-based research evaluation schemes on self-citation behaviour. *Journal of Informetrics*, 15(4), 101204.

ALLEA – All European Academies (2017). *The European Code of Conduct for Research Integrity*. https://www.allea.org/wp-content/uploads/2017/05/ALLEA-European-Code-of-Conduct-for-Research-Integrity-2017.pdf

Andersen, O. W. (2014). Some thoughts on Development Evaluation Processes. In: B. Befani, C. Barnett & E. Stern (eds). *Rethinking Impact Evaluation for Development. IDS Bulletin*, 45 (6), Brighton: Wiley Blackwell, 77–84.

Åström, F., Hammarfelt, B. & Hansson, J. (2017). Scientific publications as boundary objects: theorising the intersection of classification and research evaluation. Proceedings of the Ninth International Conference on Conceptions of Library and Information Science. Uppsala, Sweden, June, 2016, *Information Research*, 3(1), http://informationr.net/ir/22-1/colis/colis1623.html

References

Barnett, C., & Camfield, L. (2016). Ethics in evaluation. *Journal of Development Effectiveness*, 8(4), 528–534, https://doi.org/10.1080/19439342.2016.1244554

Barnett, C., & Munslow, T. (eds) (2014). Framing Ethics in Impact Evaluation: Where Are We? Which Route Should We Take? *IDS Evidence Report* 98, Brighton: IDS, https://www.cdimpact.org/publications/workshop-report-framing-ethics-impact-evaluation-where-are-we-which-route-should-we

Biagetti, M. T. et al. (2020). Ethical Theories in Research Evaluation: An Exploratory Approach. *Scholarly Assessment Reports*, 2(1), 11, https://doi.org/10.29024/sar.19

Biagioli, M., & Lippman, A. (2020). *Gaming the Metrics: Misconduct and Manipulation in Academic Research*. The MIT Press, https://doi.org/10.7551/mitpress/11087.001.0001

Bornmann, L. (2011). Scientific peer review. *Annual Review of Information Science and Technology*, 45, 197–245, https://doi.org/10.1002/aris.2011.1440450112

Bornmann, L., & Williams, R. (2020). An evaluation of percentile measures of citation impact, and a proposal for making them better. *Scientometrics*, 124, 1457–1478. DOI: 10.1007/s11192-020-03512-7

Buxton, M., & Hanney, S. (1996). How can payback from health services research be assessed? *Journal of Health Services Research & Policy*, 1(1), 35–43, https://pubmed.ncbi.nlm.nih.gov/10180843/

Constant, N., & Roberts, L. (2017). Narratives as a mode of research evaluation in citizen science: understanding broader science communication impacts. *Journal of Science Communication*, 16 (4), https://doi.org/10.22323/2.16040203

Curry, S. (2018). Let's move beyond the rhetoric: it's time to change how we judge research. *Nature*, 554 (7691), 147–147, https://doi.org/10.1038/d41586-018-01642-w

Dahler-Larsen, P. (2012). *The Evaluation Society*. Stanford, California: Stanford Business Books, https://doi.org/10.2307/j.ctvqsdq12

Daraio, C. (2017). A Framework for the Assessment of Research and Its Impacts. *Journal of Data and Information Science*, 2 (4), 7–42, https://doi.org/10.1515/jdis-2017-0018

Dawson, G., Lucocq, B., Cottrell, R., & Lewison, G. (1998). *Mapping the Landscape: National Biomedical Research Outputs 1988-95. PRISM Policy Report 9*. Wellcome Trust, https://wellcome.ac.uk/sites/default/files/wtd003187_0.pdf

De Bellis, N. (2009). *Bibliometrics and Citation Analysis from the Science Citation Index to Cybermetrics*. Scarecrow Press. DOI: 10.12775/TSB.2012.009

Elzinga, A. (1995). Reflections on research evaluation. *Science & Technology Studies*, 8 (1), 5–23.

ESF (2011). European Science Foundation, Member Organisation Forum European Peer Review Guide Integrating Policies and Practices into Coherent Procedures, https://repository.fteval.at/148/1/2011_European%20Peer%20 Review%20Guide.pdf

European Commission, Directorate-General for Research and Innovation (2017). *Interim evaluation of Horizon 202: Commission staff working document*. Publications Office, https://data.europa.eu/doi/10.2777/78199

I. Research Evaluation: What, Why, Who?

European Commission, Directorate-General for Research and Innovation. (2018). *The Open Science Policy Platform – Terms of Reference*. https://ec.europa.eu/research/opensicence/ pdf/terms_of_reference_ospp.pdf

European Commission, Directorate-General for Research and Innovation (2020). *Progress on Open Science: Towards a Shared Research Knowledge System – Final Report of the Open Science Policy Platform*. Publications Office of the European Union, https://ec.europa.eu/research/openscience/pdf/ec_rtd_ospp-final-report.pdf

Fahrenkrog, G., Polt, W., Rojo, J., Tuebke, A., Zinoecker, K., Kuhlmann, S., et al. (2002). *RTD Evaluation Toolbox – Assessing the Socio-Economic Impact of RTD-Policies*. European Commission, http://repository.fteval.at/id/eprint/272

Fanelli, D. (2020). Pressures to Publish: What Effects Do We See? In M. Biagioli & A. Lippman (eds). *Gaming the Metrics: Misconduct and Manipulation in Academic Research*. Cambridge MA, London: The MIT Press, https://doi.org/10.7551/mitpress /11087.001.0001

Fauzi, M. A., Tan, C. N. L., Daud, M., & Awalludin, M. M. N. (2020). University rankings: A review of methodological flaws. *Issues in Educational Research*, 30 (1), 79–96, http://www.iier.org.au/iier30/fauzi.pdf

Feenstra, R. A., Delgado López-Cózar, E., & Pallarés-Domínguez, D. (2021). Research Misconduct in the Fields of Ethics and Philosophy: Researchers' Perceptions in Spain. *Science and Engineering Ethics*, 27 (1), https://doi.org/10.1007/s11948-021-00278-w

Foltýnek, T., & Glendinning, I. (2015). Impact of policies for plagiarism in higher education across Europe: Results of the project. *Acta Universitatis Agriculturae et Silviculturae Mendelianae Brunensis*, 63 (1), 207–216.

Gedutis, A., & Biagetti, M. T. (2019). *Towards Ethical Principles of Research Evaluation in SSH*. RESSH project, https://ressh2019.webs.upv.es/wp-content/uploads/2019/10/ ressh_2019_paper_37.pdf

Georghiou, L., & Laredo, P. (2005). *Evaluation of publicly funded research*. Report on Berlin workshop, 26–27 September 2005. Paris: OECD.

Gibbons, M., & Johnston, R. (1974). The roles of science in technological innovation. *Research Policy*, 3 (3), 220–242, https://doi.org/10.1016/0048-7333(74)90008-0

Griliches, Z. (1958). Research Costs and Social Returns: Hybrid Corn and Related Innovations. *Journal of Political Economy*, 66, 419, https://www.journals.uchicago.ed u/doi/pdfplus/10.1086/258077

Gutzman, K. E., Bales, M. E., Belter, C. W., Chambers, T., Chan, L., Holmes, K. L., Lu, Y. L., Palmer, L. A., Reznik-Zellen, R. C., Sarli, C. C., Suiter, A. M., & Wheeler, T. R. (2018). Research evaluation support services in biomedical libraries. *Journal of medical library association*, 106 (1), dx.doi.org/10.5195/jmla.2018.205

Hammarfelt, B., & Rushforth, A. D. (2017). Indicators as judgment devices: An empirical study of citizen bibliometrics in research evaluation. *Research Evaluation*, 26 (3), 169–180, https://doi.org/10.1093/reseval/rvx018

Hanney, S. R., Gonzalez Block, M. A., Buxton, M., & Kogan, M. D. (2003). The Utilisation of Health Research in Policy-Making: Concepts, Examples and Methods of Assessment. *Health Research Policy and Systems*, 1 (1), 2. DOI: 10.1186/1478-4505-1-2

Helmer, M., Schottdorf, M., Neef, A., & Battaglia, D. (2017). Gender bias in scholarly peer review. *eLife*, 6, https://doi.org/10.7554/eLife.21718

Herbertz Benno, H., & Müller-Hill, B. (1995). Quality and efficiency of Basic Research in Molecular Biology: A Bibliometric Analysis of Thirteen Excellent Research Institutes. *Research Policy*, 24 (6), 959–979, https://doi.org/10.1016/0048-7333(94)00814-0

Herrmannova, D., & Knoth, P. (2016). Semantometrics: Towards Fulltext-based Research Evaluation. In: *Proceedings of the 16th ACM/IEEE-CS Joint Conference on Digital Libraries, 19–23 Jun 2016, Newark, New Jersey, USA*, 235–236, https://doi.org/10.1145/2910896.2925448

Hess, D. J. (1997). *Science Studies: An advanced introduction*. New York: New York University Press.

Hicks, D., Wouters, P., Waltman, L., de Rijcke, S., & Rafols, I. (2015). Bibliometrics: The Leiden Manifesto for research metrics. *Nature*, 520, 429–431. DOI: 10.1038/520429a

Hong, H. D., &Boden, M. (2003) R&D *Programme Evaluation – Theory and Practice*. Aldershot: Ashgate Publishing Limited.

Horbach, S. P. J. M., & Halffman, W. (2019). The extent and causes of academic text recycling or 'self-plagiarism'. *Research Policy*, 48 (2), 492–502. https://doi.org/10.1016/j.respol.2017.09.004

Horbach, S. P. J. M., & Halffman, W. (2019). Journal Peer Review and Editorial Evaluation: Cautious Innovator or Sleepy Giant? *Minerva*, 58 (2), 139–161, https://doi.org/10.1007/s11024-019-09388-z

INORMS Research Evaluation Working Group (2020). *Better decision making through responsible research evaluation*. Research Administration [Briefing Material], https://inorms.net/wp-content/uploads/2020/05/scope.pdf

Jewkes, J., Sawers, D., & Stillerman, R. (1958). *The Sources of Invention*. London: Macmillan.

Joint Research Centre, Institute for Prospective Technological Studies (2002). *RTD Evaluation Toolbox – Assessing the Socio-Economic Impact of RTD-Policies*. European Commission, https://repository.fteval.at/272/1/2002_RTD%20Evaluation%20Toolbox.pdf

Jurajda, Š., Kozubek, S., Münich, D., & Škoda, S. (2017). Scientific publication performance in post-communist countries: still lagging far behind. *Scientometrics*, 112 (1), 315–328, https://doi.org/10.1007/s11192-017-2389-8

Kamenetzky, A., & Hinrichs-Krapels, S. (2020). How do organisations implement research impact assessment (RIA) principles and good practice? A narrative review and exploratory study of four international research funding and administrative organisations. *Health Research Policy and Systems*, 1 (1), https://doi.org/10.1186/s12961-019-0515-1

Kara, H. (2019). The Ethics of Evaluation Research. *Research Ethics Monthly*, https://ahrecs.com/human-research-ethics/the-ethics-of-evaluation-research

I. Research Evaluation: What, Why, Who?

Kojaku, S., Livan, G., & Masuda, N. (2021). Detecting anomalous citation groups in journal networks. *Scientific Reports*, 11, 14524, https://doi.org/10.1038/s41598-021-93572-3

Kolev, I. (2017) International Philosophy Olympiad. In: Peter, M. (ed). *Encyclopedia of Educational Philosophy and Theory*. Singapore: Springer, 1158–1164.

Koley, A., & Mishra, S. (2019). Finding Citation Cartels in Academic Research. EasyChair Preprint no. 1960. https://easychair.org/publications/preprint_open/vM4b

Landsberger, H. A. (1958). *Hawthorne Revisited: Management and the Worker, Its Critics, and Developments in Human Relations in Industry*. Ithaca NY: Cornell University Press.

Lee, C. J., Sugimoto, C. R., Zhang, G., & Cronin, B. (2013). Bias in peer review. *Journal of the American Society for Information Science and Technology*, 64 (1), 2–17, https://doi.org/10.1002/asi.22784

Lee, P., West, J. D., & Howe, B. (2018). Viziometrics: Analyzing Visual Information in the Scientific Literature. *IEEE Transactions on Big Data*, 4 (1), 117–129. DOI: 10.1109/TBDATA.2017.2689038

Leigh, A. (2015, April 13). Does your compliance training make an ethical difference? *Ethical Leadership from Andrew Leigh*, https://www.ethical-leadership.co.uk/compliance-training4/

Leydesdorff, L. (2005). Evaluation of Research and Evolution of Science Indicators. *Current Science*, 89 (9), https://arxiv.org/abs/0911.4298

Mansfield, E. (1991). Academic Research and Industrial Innovation. *Research Policy*, 20 (1), 1–12, https://doi.org/10.1016/0048-7333(91)90080-A

Marjanovic, S., Hanney, S., & Wooding, S. (2009). *A historical reflection on research evaluation studies, their recurrent themes and challenges*. RAND Corporation, https://www.rand.org/content/dam/rand/pubs/technical_reports/2009/RAND_TR789.pdf

Martin, B., & Salter, B. (1996). *The relationship between public funded research and economic performance*. Science Policy Research Unit.

Milzowl, K., Reinhardt, A., Soderberg, S., & Zinocker, K. (2018). Understanding the use and usability of research evaluation studies. *Research Evaluation*, 28 (1), 94–107, https://doi.org/10.1093/reseval/rvy040

Mol, A. (2002). *The Body Multiple: Ontology in Medical Practice*. Durham, NC: Duke University Press.

Morris, M. (ed) (2008). *Evaluation Ethics for Best Practice. Cases and Commentaries*. New York: The Guilford Press.

Morris, M. (2015) Research on evaluation ethics: reflections and an agenda. In: Brandon, P. (ed). *Research on evaluation: New directions for evaluation*. Hoboken, NJ: Wiley, 31–42.

Morris, M. (2015). Research on evaluation ethics: Reflections and an agenda. *New Directions for Evaluation*, 148, 31–42.

Mustajoki, H., & Mustajoki, A. (2017). *A New Approach to Research Ethics: Using Guided Dialogue to Strengthen Research Communities*. New York: Routledge, https://doi.org/10.4324/9781315545318

Nigohosyan, D., Vutsova, A. (2018). The 2014–2020 European Regional Development Fund Indicators: The Incomplete Evolution. *Social Indicators Research*, 137, 559–577, https://doi.org/10.1007/s11205-017-1610-8

Ochsner, M., Kulczycki, E., & Gedutis, A. (2018). The Diversity of European Research Evaluation Systems. *International Conference on Science and Technology Indicators.* STI 2018 Conference proceedings, https://hdl.handle.net/1887/65217

OECD Committee on Science and Technology Policy / OECD Working Party on Innovation and Technology Policy (TIP) (2009). *Enhancing Public Research Performance through Evaluation, Impact Assessment and Priority Setting.* OECD, https://www.oecd.org/sti/inno/Enhancing-Public-Research-Performance.pdf

Office of Technology Assessment (1986). Research Funding as an Investment: Can we Measure the Return? Washington DC: US Congress, https://ota.fas.org/reports/8622.pdf

Patton, M. Q. (2014). *Evaluation Flash Cards, Embedding Evaluative Thinking in Organisational Culture.* St Paul, MN: Otto Bremer Foundation.

Penfield, T., Baker, M. J., Scoble, R., & Wykes, M. C. (2014). Assessment, evaluations, and definitions of research impact: A review. *Research Evaluation*, 23 (1), https://doi.org/10.1093/reseval/rvt021

Perez, O., Bar-Ilan, J., Cohen, R., & Schreiber, N. (2019). The Network of Law Reviews: Citation Cartels, Scientific Communities, and Journal Rankings. *Modern Law Review*, 82, 2, 240–268, https://doi.org/ 10.1111/1468-2230.12405

Pleger, L., & Sager, F. (2018). Betterment, undermining, support and distortion: A heuristic model for the analysis of pressure on evaluators. *Evaluation and Program Planning*, 69, 166–172. DOI: 10.1016/j.evalprogplan.2016.002

Research evaluation needs to change with the times [Editorial] (2022). *Nature*, 601, 166, https://doi.org/10.1038/d41586-022-00056-z

Rijcke, S., & Stöckelová, T. (2020). Predatory Publishing and the Imperative of International Productivity: Feeding Off and Feeding Up the Dominant. In M. Biagioli & A. Lippman (eds). *Gaming the Metrics: Misconduct and Manipulation in Academic Research.* Cambridge MA, London: The MIT Press, https://doi.org/10.7551/mitpress/ 11087.001.0001

Rivera, H. (2018). Inappropriate Authorship and Kinship in Research Evaluation. *Journal of Korean Medical Science*, 33 (13), https://doi.org/10.3346/jkms.2018.33.e105

Ronda-Pupo, G. A. (2017). Research evaluation of author's citation-based performance through the relative author superiority index. *Transinformação*, 29 (2), http://dx.doi.org/10.1590/2318-08892017000200006

Rossi, P. H., & Freeman, H. (1999). *Evaluation: A Systematic Approach.* Thousand Oaks CA: Sage Publications.

San Francisco Declaration on Research Assessment (DORA). https://sfdora.org/read/

Rouet, G. (2022) (ed) *Classement des universités. Lectures, publications reçues.* Paris : CNRS éditions.

Schwandt, T. A. (2015). *Evaluation Foundations Revisited: Cultivating a Life of the Mind for Practice.* Stanford: Stanford University Press.

Schwandt, T. A. (2018). Acting together in determining value: A professional ethical responsibility of evaluators. *Evaluation*, 24 (3), 306–317, https://doi.org/10.1177/1356389018781362

Sherwin, C. W., & Isenson, R. S. (1967). Project Hindsight. *Science*, 156 (3782), 1571–1577. DOI: 10.1109/science.156.3782.1571

Strielkowski, W., Gryshova, I., & Shcherbata, M. (2017). Predatory Publishing and Beall's List: Lessons for the Countries Adapting Novel Research Evaluation Criteria. *Science and education*, 8, 39–43, https://doi.org/10.24195/2414-4665-2017-8-5

Szomszor, M., Adams, J., Fry, R., Gebert, C., Pendlebury, D. A., Potter, R. W. K., & Rogers, G. (2021). Interpreting Bibliometric Data. *Frontiers in Research Metrics and Analytics*, 5:628703. DOI: 10.3389/frma.2020.628703

Thomas, D. A., Nedeva, M., Tirado, M. M., & Jacob, M. (2020). Changing research on research evaluation: A critical literature review to revisit the agenda. *Research Evaluation*, 29 (3), 275–288, https://doi.org/10.1093/reseval/rvaa008

Thomas, R. (2018). *Questioning the Assessment of Research Impact Illusions, Myths and Marginal Sectors*. Springer, https://doi.org/10.1007/978-3-319-95723-4

Thurtle, P., & Mitchell, R. (2002). *Semiotic Flesh: Information and the Human Body*. Seattle: University of Washington Press.

Tusting, K. (2018). The genre regime of research evaluation: contradictory systems of value around academics' writing. *Language and Education*, 32 (6), 477–493, https://doi.org/10.1080/09500782.2018.1505905

Vutsova, A. (2006). *Research Evaluation – Bulgarian Case, Bulgarian Integration into Europe & NATO*. Zvezdi.

Vutsova, A. (2009a). Science and Innovations within the International Cooperation in Europe. *Economic Thought*, 4, 77–89, https://www.ceeol.com/search/article-detail?id=69469

Vutsova, A. (2009b). *Research Policy in the Context of European Integration*. Sofia: Technical University.

Vutsova, A. (2014). *Influence of the EU Instruments on the Institutional Development of Higher Education and Science*. Zvezdi.

Waltman, L., Calero-Medina, C., Kosten, J., Noyons, E. C. M., Tijssen, R. J. W., & van Eck, N. J. (2012). The Leiden ranking 2011/2012: data collection, indicators, and interpretation. *Journal of the Association for Information Science and Technology*, 63 (12), 2419–2432. DOI: 10.1002/asi.22708

Weinberg, A. M. (1989). Criteria for Evaluation, a Generation later. In D. Evered & S. Narnett (eds). *Evaluation of Scientific Research*. Ciba Foundation Conference.

Whitley, R. (2007). Changing Governance of the Public Sciences. The Consequences of Establishing Research Evaluation Systems for Knowledge Production in Different Countries and Scientific Field. In R. Whitley & J. Gläser (eds). *The Changing Governance of the Sciences. The Advent of Research Evaluation Systems*. Dordrecht: Springer, 3–27.

Williams, A. E. (2017). Altmetrics: an overview and evaluation. *Online Information Review*, 41 (3), 311–317, https://doi.org/10.1108/OIR-10-2016-0294

Williams, L. (2016). Ethics in international development evaluation and research: what is the problem, why does it matter and what can we do about it? *Journal of Development Effectiveness*, 8 (4), 535–552. DOI: 10.1080/19439342.2016.1244700

Wilsdon, J., Allen, L., Belfiore, E., Campbell, P., Curry, S., Hill, S., Jones, R., Kain, R., Kerridge, S., Thelwall, M., Tinkler, J., Viney, I., Wouters, P., Hill, J., & Johnson, B. (2015). *The Metric Tide: Report of the Independent Review of the Role of Metrics in Research Assessment and Management*. HEFCE. DOI: 10.13140/RG.2.1.4929.1363

Wooding, S., Anton, S., Grant, J., Hanney, S., Hoorens, S., Lierens, A., Shergold, M., & Venema, M. (2004). *The Returns from Arthritis Research. Volume 2: The Case Studies*. RAND Corporation, https://www.rand.org/pubs/technical_reports/TR176.html

World Conferences on Research Integrity (2019). *Hong Kong Principles for assessing researchers*, https://wcrif.org/guidance/hong-kong-principles

Wouters, P. (2020). The Mismeasurement of Quality and Impact. In M. Biagioli & A. Lippman (eds). *Gaming the Metrics: Misconduct and Manipulation in Academic Research*. Cambridge MA, London: The MIT Press, https://doi.org/10.7551/mitpress/11087.001.0001

Zhang, L., Rousseau, R., & Sivertsen, G. (2017). Science deserves to be judged by its contents, not by its wrapping: Revisiting Seglen's work on journal impact and research evaluation. *PLoS ONE*, 12 (3), Article e0174205, https://doi.org/10.1371/journal.pone.0174205

Zubascu, F. (2018) Poland's 'Constitution for Science' gives universities more power and accountability. *ScienceBusiness*, November 20, 2018, https://sciencebusiness.net/news/polands-constitution-science-gives-universities-more-power-and-accountability

II. Research Impact Assessment

1. Impact assessment – General definition

The routes of impact assessment could be traced back to the cross-impact assessment proposed by Gordon and Helmer in 1966 (Gordon, 1994), the environmental impact statements since 1970 (National Environmental Policy Act), and technology assessments (Coates, 1971). All these methods of futures studies aimed to develop plausible scenarios and strategies to cope with the growing uncertainty.

The impact assessment is an ongoing process of monitoring and analysing the social, economic, and ecological changes which occur as a result of the implementation of a given activity. The objectives of an impact assessment are usually aligned with the functions of a given organisation, and in specific cases they are independent of regulatory factors (ecological assessments are an exception, for example). The impact assessments usually look beyond the standard horizon of planning of the activities.

An impact assessment usually surpasses the boundaries of the 'gross' results and impacts foreseen in a given policy, programme, project, or initiative. Sometimes impact assessments are conducted within the larger context of foresight studies, which are trying to back-cast what should be done in order to reach a desirable future or to avoid undesirable one. The time-horizons are always extending and the overall uncertainty grows, thus calling for foresight-based capacity to react to uncertainty shocks. The impact assessment could be considered also as a part of broader agenda of 'evidence-based policy making'. It also can be used to measure programmes implementation alternatives and their innovativeness.

In general, 'impact assessment' deals with the effects of proposed and/or planned actions (Porter & Rossini, 2019). The International Association for Impact Assessment (Fargo, North Dakota, USA) accepts that the impact assessment is the process of identifying the future consequences of a current or proposed action through which social justice and quality of the environment are achieved to a certain extent. According to this association, the impact assessment is one of the approaches for analysing policies and programmes, and is also complemented by a technological assessment and a risk assessment (International Association for Impact Assessment). Impact assessments (IA) should be participatory, i.e. engaging all stakeholders, and independent from the programme sponsor. At the same time impacts could differ substantially (academic impact as the intellectual contribution to the field, economic effect on direct users of the research, and various indirect socio-economic effects).

According to the European Commission, the impact assessment "must identify and describe the problem to be tackled, establish objectives, formulate policy options, assess the impacts of these options and describe how the expected results will be monitored" (European Commission, Directorate-General for Research and Innovation, 2017). This process provides decision-makers with data regarding the advantages and disadvantages of the various proposed solutions on the basis of their potential impacts.

In some countries, manuals have been developed to assess the impact on regulations, as they are a tool which contributes to the formulation and implementation of better public policies. In this way, the process of making better and better decisions (operational, strategic, normative) is improved. Strategic decisions have a lasting effect in the long run and their implementation has a transformative effect on society. The principles IA adheres to are transparency, reasonableness, efficiency, and effectiveness. The handbooks on preparing an impact assessment are defined as a tool for examining the effects of different versions of actions aimed at resolving existing issues from the point of view of costs, benefits, and related risks.

The impact assessment cannot be categorically referred to only one of the stages of the public policies cycle. Elements of it can be found in the development of policies, the formulation of the objectives thereof, the decision-making process, and the analysis and assessment of these decisions. There are both scientific and purely practical justifications for such a diffusion.

The European Commission, Directorate-General for Research and Innovation (2017) proposes seven consecutive analytical steps for implementing the impact assessment:

1. Definition of the problem;
2. Clarification of the policy objectives;
3. Proposal of alternative options;
4. Examination of the economic, social and ecological impacts;
5. Comparison of the options;
6. Proposal of a preferred option;
7. Definition of monitoring and assessment indicators/procedures.

1. Impact assessment – General definition

The impact assessment incorporates the advantages of both the rational and the incremental decision-making model in order to achieve a combined search for decisions or decision-making (Etzioni, 2001).

The regulatory impact assessment is proposed and developed as a tool by the Organisation for Economic Co-operation and Development (OECD Committee on Science and Technology Policy / OECD Working Party on Innovation and Technology Policy (TIP), 2009), and it is used for better regulation in the context of the economic policies. This assessment aims to improve the effectiveness and efficiency of governments so that they can improve competitiveness and economic results in the innovative and globalised economy.

The impact assessment of a given policy originates from the concepts of environmental protection, sustainable development, and environmental rights of citizens. At the end of the 20th century a number of countries introduced this approach in the analysis of some sectoral policies such as construction, transport, energy, agriculture, etc. This is an assessment of the long-term impact of people's business activity on the environmental components. Later on, the impact assessment was extended to other policies, unbounded to ecology, for instance horizontal ones (education, science, communication).

The impact assessment is recognised equally well by the entities financing certain activities (donors) and by the entities responsible for implementing programmes, because both sides can learn what the expected results are and improve the effectiveness and efficiency of their work.

As a conceptual framework, the impact assessment has three main elements:

- impact chain model;
- specification of the levels on which the impacts are assessed;
- definition of the types of impacts which have to be assessed.

According to some authors (Tran & Daim, 2008; Newson et al., 2018), an important aspect of the impact assessment concept is the choice of suitable methods and the development of tools for data analysis. Qualitative tools are suitable for the analysis of the processes, while quantitative research and analytical methods are used for checking achievements and impacts. The following qualitative methods are frequently used:

- secondary analysis of existing data;
- management (semi-structured) interviews;

- standardised (structured) interviews;
- model research.

The question which methods to choose depends on the task and the objectives of the assessment, but as a whole the qualitative and quantitative research methods have to be combined.

For example, when analysing the objectives of a project and the interventions thereof, the data from the project documentation has to be analysed. The results from these analyses shall be used to trace the anticipated effects against the objectives or the degree to which they are achieved.

In the case of counterfactual impact assessments, facts and opposing assumptions are compared with the aim of looking for an answer to the question 'What would have happened, if...?'. When we consider whether to introduce a new policy or to attempt to assess to what extent a given pilot programme has been successful, we look at a variety of opposing questions: 'What if the policy was introduced?', 'What if the policy did not exist?' (Cartwright, 2003).

Counterfactual analyses are based on the idea that, in order to determine the net effect (contribution) of a given policy, programme, or intervention, the assessment has to be constructed on an inexistent (counterfactual) situation in which this intervention was not conducted. The assessment of the net effect is based on the assumption that every reason on its own can influence the result, i.e., it is accepted that the reasons are independent and complementary as an effect (Ragin & Sonnett, 2005).

The 'difference-in-differences' approach applied in the impact assessment suggests the presence of data about the results of two control groups, an experimental one and a control group, before and after a given intervention, regardless of the fact that this is applicable to the counterfactual analysis as a whole. In order to apply this method, data about the beneficiaries and non-beneficiaries is needed before and after the intervention (EVALSED, 2013). The following is examined:

- difference between beneficiaries and non-beneficiaries;
- difference (between beneficiaries and non-beneficiaries) in the period before receiving support and after that.

The 'propensity score matching' approach aims to eliminate the impact of side factors through control on the characteristics which describe the units in the experimental and the control group.

'Contribution analysis' is another approach for measuring the results and is widely used in the financial assessment of business activities and products and, to a lesser extent, in other fields such as analysis of a media campaign, medicine, ecology, etc. According to Mayne (1999), the 'contribution analysis' is characterised by the following specificities:

- identification of issues by measuring the specific contribution of a given programme with regards to what has been achieved, and mainly reporting the impact of other factors;
- analysis and presentation of the logic behind the programme through logic models which trace the cause-effect relations and identify important external factors;
- identification, measurement and documentation of the expected changes in behaviour;
- use of indicators which can help determine the contribution of a given intervention;
- tracking the implementation over time or the location by searching for an answer to sample questions: Are the results achieved after the intervention?, Do the results disappear after ending the intervention?, Are the biggest results achieved?, etc.;
- examination and discussion of possible alternative explanations;
- collection of additional data;
- review and confirmation of the contribution (Mayne, 2008).

Apart from the above-mentioned approaches, practice has established the application of some econometrics. For example, the 'discontinuity design' approach is applied in the cases where there is a threshold/condition for participation in a given policy.

In practice, a lot of assessments establish whether a result has been achieved and, if yes, what is the role of the programme analysed in this. In order to determine the contribution of a given programme, it is important to see what advantages and added value have been demonstrated and whether they provide an opportunity to make decisions regarding its future development (Mayne, 2001).

Some of the impact assessment models allow for a factor and regression analysis in view of searching for the degree of impact of different factors on individual indicators of specific systems (for example, the higher education system). However, they are rarely applied to the scientific research system in particular.

In logic models there are elements which are linked in a standard succession:

- **inputs/resources** – human, financial, organisational resources which are going to be invested in a particular programme;
- **activities** – projects/interventions/measures, which are foreseen under a given programme;
- **outputs** – direct outputs of a given programme which shall contribute to achieving outcomes;
- **outcomes** – a change in the condition of persons, institutions or territories;
- **impact** – impact means a long-term change in the condition of persons, institutions, or territories.

Typical for these models is that they not only recreate cause-effect relations but also deal with specific categories and create a specific framework. In this sense, when using logic models, the grouping of elements of a given programme is just as important as tracking the cause-effect relations.

Process Monitoring of Impacts (PMI) (Hummelbrunner, 2006) is based on the 'results monitoring' approach. The key characteristic of this concept is that it does not follow the usual cause-effect relations but rather focuses on the importance of beneficiaries and the target groups for achieving the expected effects (Earl et al. 2001). This approach is a combination of concepts which have been initially developed for programmes in developing countries and have subsequently been adapted to the needs for monitoring projects or programmes in the field of structured policy. The main assumption on which the method is based is that the inputs and the outputs have to be used in order to achieve the desired effect. An advantage of the PMI approach is that it examines the resources and the achievement of the effects in a dynamic way, and it takes into account that it is necessary for them to be used by specific stakeholders in order to reach the objectives of a given programme. The external factors are also considered as a key element, but in some cases there is a possibility that the relation between outcomes and impact may be unclear (Nigohosyan & Vutsova, 2018).

2. The assessment of scientific research and its impact on higher education systems and horizontal research organisations

2.1. Importance of research assessment for universities

Over the past few decades, an increase in the number of universities (private and public) has been observed (predominant in EU and more detailed in new member states (NMC) and associated countries (ACs)). They have a different coverage in terms of resources, scale, and mission (Martin, 2012; Watts, 2017).

To a certain degree this increase is a result of the Bologna Process. On the one hand, it equated the master's degrees of universities and vocational colleges such as Fachhochschulen (FHS), making it possible for magistrates from these Higher Education Institutions (HEI) to transfer to a university and develop a doctoral thesis (FHS usually does not offer doctorates); on the other hand, the pursuit of open mobility – one from the postulates of the Bologna Process – influences the increase in the number of HEI seeking partnership with European universities. The Bologna Process initiated transformation processes regarding legislative changes, simplification of the procedures for opening new HEI structures, entry of private investments into this process, etc., which also contributed to the increase in the number of universities.

The latest trends in relation to the market-oriented development of the higher education system show changes compared to the classic understanding of what a university is. In the context of a global economic environment, universities compete to attract students, staff, and income, and the latter comes from different financial resources: fees, preferential transfers, research grants, etc. On the other hand, the official results presented (obtained from audits or annual reports), which concern teaching, research, and employability of the alumni, allow users to be informed through different rankings in order to make an informed decision on the basis of the quality offered and the price requested. This forces universities to apply a management approach similar to the corporate one (Buckland, 2009; Hemsley-Brown & Oplatka, 2010; Ayikoru et al., 2009).

Those universities which are natural research centres are perceived as an inseparable part of the regional, national, and international economies. This is why evidence has to be presented to ascertain their contribution to specific economic results. Therefore, in order to justify publicly financed studies, they have to generate impact which leads to an improvement in the economic or social environment (Brown & Carasso, 2013; Gaffikin & Perry, 2009).

The market approach applied to higher education requires an 'effective' management of universities. A lot of publications (Lasakova et al., 2017; Orr, 1997; Naudé & Ivy, 1999) state that the fate of individual universities depends on management which has to plan adequate activities and make strategic investments. At the same time, the productivity of lecturers (research 'outcomes', the quality of teaching, and other aspects of their work) have to be comparable with their competitors' outcomes.

Some researchers find that the modern corporate management of universities threatens 'academic freedom' and reduces collegiality (Thomas 2018; Williams 2016). The result from the general understanding of the 'achievements' and the presence of benchmarking indicators creates conditions for some lecturers to be very successful, while for others there is an increased sense of failure (Clarke & Knights, 2015). Moreover, the need for 'quality delivery' creates potentially damaging consequences, including in ethical terms. For example, the same data are used in different ways by the same researchers in order to be presented to different types of audiences (Thomas, 2018).

The penetration of international financial flows in research centres, intended for the implementation of research activities and the subsequent effects from the 'impact', concerns not only academic researchers but the management bodies of the main structures as well. For the latter, the reputation of the institution is very important and is related to its ability to perform well in research assessment. Universities aim to increase their results as much as possible and take leading positions in world rankings (Yudkevich et al. 2016). For academics, the career development perspectives are influenced not only by the ability of a given researcher to publish and attract research grants but also by his/her ability to generate impact (Bastow et al. 2014).

Research financing systems which are results-based do not usually differentiate their assessment approach with regards to disciplines or research fields (Hicks, 2012) though there are significant differences between disciplines, and there is also the so-called non-academic impact (Bastow et al., 2014). Public agencies financing research and research organisations bear a great responsibility for a more comprehensive impact of the studies which they support financially. Regardless of the fact that there are tools for research impact assessment, little is known and shared about how these organisations apply these activities in practice.

Despite the need for accountability on the part of organisations which finance different scientific research, there is not enough information about how such an assessment is performed in practice within research organisations. Kamenetzky and Hinrichs-Krapels (2020) believe that there is no empirical basis for impact assessment of institutional policies, especially in relation to structures financing scientific research. Research organisations play an important role in determining the impact assessment procedures, but they are not efficient enough, because the materials published on this topic lack data and recommendations about the practical application in the context of complex research financing systems (Kamenetzky & Hinrichs-Krapels, 2020).

Non-academic impact is studied in more detail where universities with contrasting missions (Hewitt-Dundas, 2012) and their relations with knowledge-intensive industrial sectors are analysed (Banal-Estanol et al., 2015; Bozeman et al., 2013, 2015). Other scholars study the links of universities with sectors which do not require a high qualification (Thomas & Ormerod 2017) and believe that greater control should be exercised over the dynamic of research impact in different contexts (Thomas, 2018). They also presume that academic researchers are too busy applying different strategies for disseminating their work (Marchant, 2017) at the expense of their academic independence and critical approach (Watermeyer, 2016).

3. Methods for assessing research impact

Studying assessment practices is important for a number of reasons. A big part of research literature which studies the impact of scientific research is theoretical in nature, and the term 'impact' is comprehensive. Even though there are models and tools for assessing research impact, the guidelines as to what works and for whom are limited.

Benefits of research would go beyond the academia over a number of different areas, visualised in Figure 2.1. Usually researchers have to plan activities specifically related to enhancing impact.

II. Research Impact Assessment

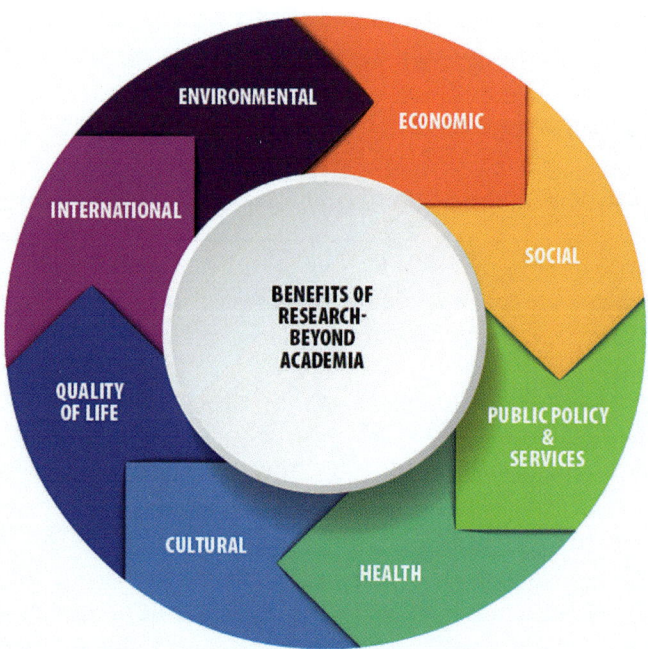

Source: Adapted from The University of Sheffield, Research Services, https://www.sheffield.ac.uk/rs/impact/pathways.

Figure 2.1: Benefits of Research beyond academia

Impact assessment of scientific research is a difficult task and has to take into consideration political and socio-economic factors. This type of impact assessment usually has four main objectives:

(1) **Performance** – to allow universities and research organisations to monitor and manage their performance and to consciously disseminate the results and contribution to their local, national, and international communities.
(2) **Accountability** – to demonstrate the social and economic value of the performed research to the government, stakeholders, and the wider public. Governments aim to report (justify and legitimise) the spending of public funds by demonstrating their contribution with regards to socio-economic benefits to tax payers, voters, and society (European Science Foundation, 2009; Davies et al., 2005; Nutley & Walter 2005; Hanney & Gonzalez-Block, 2011).

3. Methods for assessing research impact

(3) **Informed financing** – to become aware of the socio-economic value of the research and to consequently make an informed decision for a given financing. Assessing the research contribution could facilitate better targeting of the future financing which will allow specific areas to achieve the desired impact. As Donovan (2011) comments, the impact assessment is a powerful tool for creating evidence-based actions on the part of the governments for the purpose of a strengthened research support.

(4) **Understanding** – to make sense of the method and the ways in which research leads to or would lead to impacts, and to develop better methods for achieving impact.

Clear presentation of the impact from research may allow for accountability before financing organisations and consumers (Kelly & McNicoll, 2011).

Hinrichs-Krapels and Grant explore the effectiveness, efficiency and equity (3Es) of research impact assessment. On the figure below the 3Es are illustrated. Inputs, process, outputs, and outcomes of the research process are shown. The authors view research equity as aligned with wider impact to certain social goals such as inclusion and equality. They believe that research assessment is necessary to achieve such equity.

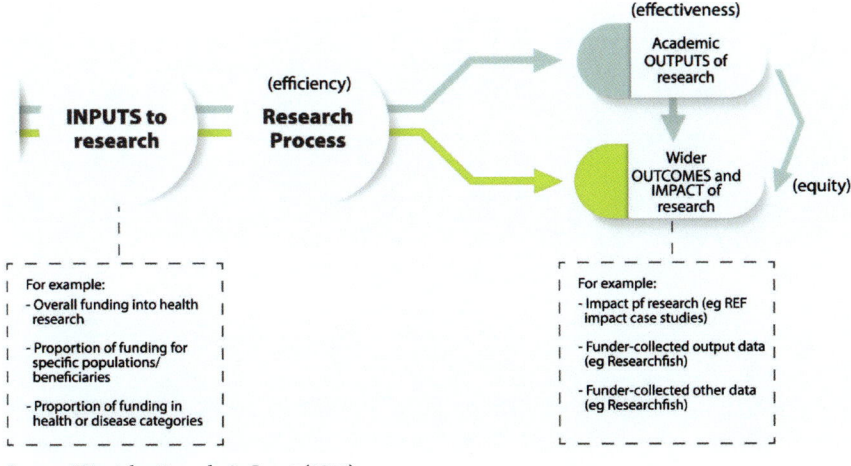

Source: Hinrichs-Krapels & Grant (2016).

Figure 2.2: Essential inputs, outputs, outcomes, and impact of the research process

Impact assessments are not acceptable for some researchers because they mainly focus on disciplines and topics where the impact can be easily proven and can be validated from an economic point of view. This type of approach may lead to a certain devaluation of the significance of fundamental scientific research. Understanding what impact there is in different fields of a given study and appreciating the diversity of indicators used as evidence is necessary for achieving a reasonable assessment.

Some authors (Joly & Matt, 2017) believe that more recent approaches towards research impact assessment take into consideration the complex and interactive nature of innovation and shift towards addressing societal needs. The following figure represents simplified impact pathways of research according to Belcher (2021). The main aim of research in general is to generate new knowledge and innovation, which has its impact through the different spheres of control, influence, and interest. New knowledge and innovation lead to changes in stakeholders and policies and, eventually, to social, economic, and/or environmental transformation. All processes are underlined by monitoring, evaluation, and learning as integral part of achieving real impact. In addition, stakeholder engagement is highlighted as a continuous process.

3. Methods for assessing research impact

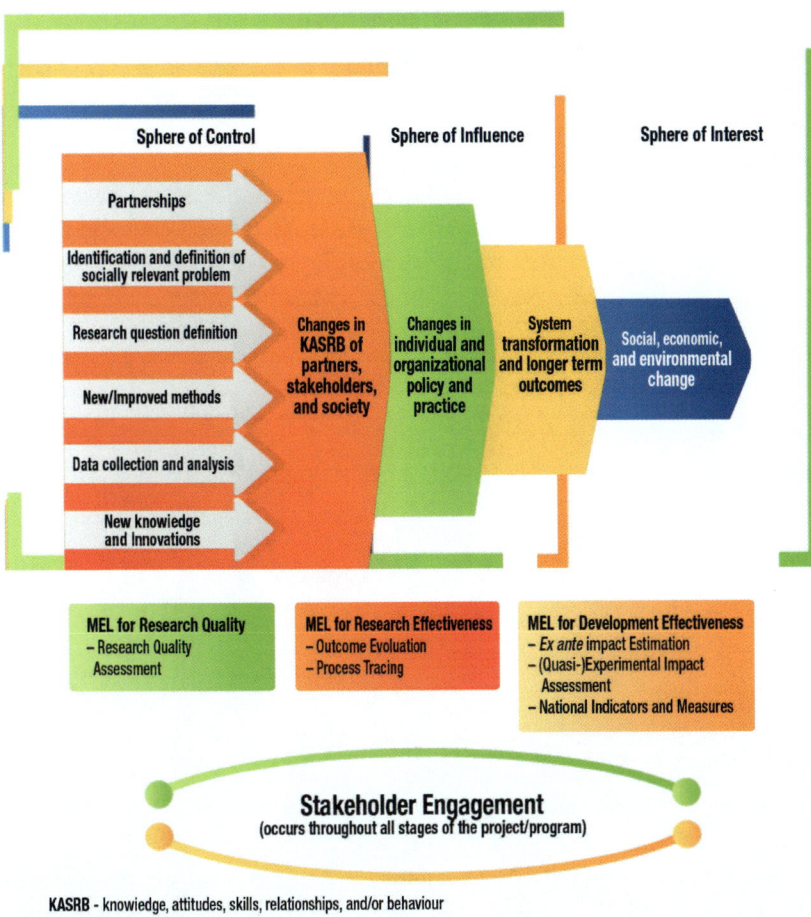

Source: Belcher (2021).

Figure 2.3: Research to impact pathways

Bibliometrics can be used to demonstrate the benefits of scientific research in the academic environment, and they are often part of a larger impact spectrum observed on an international level. For example, within Excellence in Research for Australia and the use of Star Metrics in the USA, quantitative measures are applied for the purpose of assessing impact, publications, citation, and revenue from scientific research. These 'traditional' bibliometrics can be perceived only as an element of the full impact (Bornmann & Marx, 2013) without reflecting the cause-effect relation. Some authors (Vonortas & Link, 2012) believe that the standard approaches, which are actively used in the assessment of research programmes, such as studies, cases, bibliometrics, econometrics and statistical analyses, content analysis, and expert evaluation, have certain shortcomings with regards to measuring impact.

The assessment which reflects a wider socio-economic impact uses a new type of indicators, such as registered intellectual property and generated trade income (Australian Research Council, 2009). In the UK, impact assessments which study bigger socio-economic benefits were applied for the first time in the field of biomedical and health sciences (Grant, 2006) – fields which have the ambition to justify the significant investment they have received.

Impact assessment frameworks have been developed and are being applied, taking into account the specific requirements of the organisation and the stakeholders. This is the reason why a lot of different impact assessment models are on offer. Some of the most popular models which demonstrate a contrast in the approaches available are the following:

Penfield (2014) describes several models related to impact assessment.

- The Payback Framework. Buxton and Hanney formulated the model at Brunel University at the end of the 20th century. Penfield (2014) recognises it as one of the most often applied approaches for impact assessment. The model uses healthcare field and includes an impact assessment of academic results and benefits for the society (Donovan & Hanney, 2011). As described by Hanney and Gonzalez-Block (2011), the payback framework model systematically links research to the benefits thereof and can be examined at two levels. The first level correlates specific research results and their potential for dissemination, as a general framework for assessing the overall research impact. The second level refers to a multidimensional classification scheme, which allows the assessment of the various research outputs, outcomes, and impacts. The method continues to be of interest and discussed by researchers (Rollins et al., 2020).
- Social Impact Assessment Methods for research and funding instruments through the study of Productive Interactions (SIAMPI). The model is a result of the Dutch project 'Evaluating Research in Context'. It aims to assess the social impact of academic work analysing different research areas (Spaapen et al., 2011). This approach enables a more in-depth understanding of social impact through a focused examination of the

links between the (involved) researchers. It studies formal and informal networks formed amongst scientists. However, the method is relevant only for assessing specific research aspects.
- Research Quality Framework (RQF). The approach is one of the first attempts to evaluate the quality and socio-economic impact of scientific research in Australia. The government aimed to construct a framework to distribute funds for research in a justifiable way. Researchers used a case study to demonstrate the economic, social, ecological, and cultural impact of their work, then checked by an expert group (Duryea et al., 2007). Such assessment was piloted on the Australian Technology Network, and the authors believed that qualitative and quantitative evidence was gathered. However, more recently the method was criticised because it was based on assessing non-academic impact and because of aspects of its methodology (Gunn & Mintrom, 2018).

There is no consensus on the topic of measuring impact assessment, and different national systems are still looking for the best combination of criteria, varying from method to method. For instance, both national Bulgarian instruments, contributing to research and innovation activities, are based on competition but apply different approaches. While the National Research Fund operates mainly with quantitative measures such as publications, citations, etc., thus outlining academic impact only, the National Innovation Fund aims to assess full impact and measure predominately socio-economic impact, neglecting to some extend academic impact. In addition, the set of applicable criteria is not balanced very well. Some quasi approaches are applied to national research programmes, where elements of socio-economic impact are part of binding criteria. But there is not enough data from evaluation due to the fact that the national programmes have been reported the first performed period only.

The BETA-EvaRIO method aims to assess the impact of different aspects of research infrastructure (Bach & Wolff, 2017). It focuses on specific groups of actors and the relationship between types of effects – effects on performance, capacity effects, direct and indirect effects. Its benefits lie in combining qualitative and quantitative tools and various types of metrics from diverse sources; in this way the consistency of results is ensured.

The START programme in Austria proved to be quite successful for researchers starting their careers. To assess the results, the evaluators of the programme applied mixed approaches, for example surveys and case studies, with the goal to overcome the limitations of the individual ones.

Again, quantitative and qualitative data were used, relying on different sources (Seus & Bührer, 2017).

Some prospective impact assessment practices include general equilibrium models, data links, scientometrics, indicators based on research and in combination with econometric analyses, and case studies. These different methodologies are still developing, but they have set the foundation for a new type of research.

The scope and diversity of the developed frameworks demonstrate the difference in the objective of the assessment and the type of expected impact. Studies on econometric benefits from biomedical and health research (Penfield et al., 2014) show that the different methodologies provide different approaches for establishing those benefits. There is still a big discussion on the benefits and shortcomings of a number of assessment tools (bibliometrics, economic norm of return on investment, reviewing, case study, logic-based modelling, and comparative analysis), which are examined in detail by Grant (2006). To assess the impact of research at different levels – micro, meso, and macro at the same time – and to scale-up the results remains a challenge (Jolly & Matt, 2017).

4. Social impact of research

Despite the fact that there was a prolonged period devoted to the development of methodologies for measuring and assessing research impact, there are still gaps with regards to the techniques applied.

Social impact criteria can be formulated in different ways, as illustrated in Figure 2.4.

4. Social impact of research

Source: Adapted from Sorde (2015).

Figure 2.4: Social impact criteria

The main issue with regards to understanding the impact on the social environment is the lack of satisfactory analytical tools to monitor the cause-effect relation and the scale of the effects of research on social changes.

Economic assessments of scientific research and technologies usually fall into two related categories: social norm of return on investment and analysis of the collective output. The approaches with regards to the social norm for return on investment can be used in a different context and aim to evaluate the social benefits accumulated from the technological changes by linking the value of the intended benefits with the price of the investments made. Measuring the social norm for return on investment is most often done by using the analysis of costs and benefits in order to make an assessment at project and programme level (for example, Link, 1996a, 1996b; Ruegg, 1996; Audretsch et al., 2002; Saavedra & Bozeman, 2004). The second category – analysis of the collective output – has an impact on the formulation of economic development policies. This category is usually focused on the contribution of technologies to the national or regional economy (for example, see Solow, 1957).

Despite their many advantages, the methods based on economic assessment show limitations with regards to measuring the social impact of scientific research. The methods based on cost-benefit or a percentage of return on investments only give a limited idea about the creation of research capacity or the transformative aspects of the research. They are largely focused on the specific products of research projects such as articles in journals or sellable products. Such a focus is best applied when there are specific limitations (for example, a research and development project). The assessments which are based on an economic approach are usually static, despite the efforts to examine future benefits. They rarely take into account the changes which appear in the 'products' that are being evaluated and even more rarely the changes in institutions or the human resources which have produced them. In addition, many of the social acquisitions and costs for science and technologies are not well evaluated in financial terms.

While it is possible to identify the difficulties in conducting a valid assessment of the end social impacts of a given research, it is not possible to measure them completely. The studies conducted show that often only one factor for measuring social results is identified, and it is rarely among the most significant ones. Regardless of whether the standard economic-based approaches, such as cost-benefit analysis, monitoring of social indicators, social accounting, or model studies of cases, are used, the clear definition of the cause-effect relation for complex social impacts is always difficult.

Determining and measuring the various benefits for society from investments in scientific research is not an easy task. This is due to the fact that a lot of key scientific discoveries have been made by accident ('serendipity'), and a lot of applications of scientific research have found a place in fields which are different to the initial intention of researchers. Moreover, the time needed to generate all benefits from publicly financed research activities may be very long, and so in specific cases measuring the impacts may be inaccurate because it is premature and/or partial. Last but not least, non-economic impacts from research are more difficult to measure. For example, measuring health results is not an easy process; thus, it complicates the efforts to link health results to public investments in scientific research and development. Similar difficulties occur with regards to the investments in research aimed at the national security sector.

The econometric analysis of the link between research activity and the results thereof is usually based on the concept of linear innovation. Presumably, part of the innovations could start from basic research followed by applicable ones and end with the production and dissemination of new products and processes in the economy. It is common knowledge, however, that innovations are linked to different participants in the process, they are the result of a mixture of public and private investments, trade interests, and many other factors. Innovations require a more comprehensive approach for measuring and analysing the economic and social impacts.

It would be useful to realise the significance of impact assessments with regards to decision-makers, while ensuring that the assessment methods and indicators applied take into account the changing environment, the increasing number of stakeholders and the level of intersectoral coordination. Increasing stakeholders' trust in the impact assessment is also important and could be improved through their conscious inclusion in the early stages of the process (OECD, 2009).

Over the past few years, researchers and governments have become interested in the non-economic impacts of publicly financed scientific research. There is a certain degree of consensus among researchers that one of the first steps towards a better understanding of the non-economic impacts is to determine a framework which links the investments and the well-being of a given country (Sharpe & Smith, 2005). Cozzens (2007) claims that the indicators for social results from research are neither difficult, nor rare, and are related to the public objectives of the research. According to her, what is missing are not results indicators but the logic which links them to scientific research and innovations.

The question about the typology of the impact should be defined in more detail by examining not only the social impact, for example, but the economic, non-economic, health impact, etc. Figure 2.5 presents an analysis of the effects which are linked to the main representatives involved in the process.

Sharpe and Smith (2005) develop a common framework for assessing the impact of research on the well-being of a given nation. This framework (Figure 2.5) links investments with the well-being, where the latter is measured by the increased knowledge of social actors generated by the scientific research conducted. Generally speaking, this common framework can be applied to different types of financial studies the results of which are used by different social actors and which influence different factors of well-being (OECD, 2009). The approach includes examining the results in three aspects: economic, social, and environmental.

II. Research Impact Assessment

Source: Sharpe & Smith (2005).

Figure 2.5: Framework for analysis of the effects of research on well-being

5. Practical comments

Quality of impact assessments depend significantly on adequate selection of target groups to be studied. Then a gap analysis should be conducted identifying existing deficits, their significance, and to what extent the state intervention is suitable in such cases. Since state intervention may gradually change the behaviour of the stakeholders in different ways (negative or positive), it should be determined which of the methods used are still suitable.

By taking into account the fact that each national innovations system is to a certain extent unique and the impact assessment methods cannot be universally applied, it is advisable to highlight part of the problems and the possible solutions which have been identified. For example, there are difficulties related to achieving the expectations of all stakeholders (a result from the dynamic environment and the increasing number of stakeholders). The discrepancy between the stakeholders' objectives can be a reason why some initiatives may either fail or lead to the best possible results and/or solutions. There is a need for an adequate development of a new policy based on the impact assessment and a better understanding of the motivation and the possible behaviour of the stakeholders.

The combination of different methods and the inclusion of a number of stakeholders in the assessment process can help overcome the individual shortcomings of the various approaches. Not all assessments use clear and time-consistent efficiency indicators, and the integration of the field-related specificities is not transparent in most cases.

The policy with regards to determining the scientific research programmes and the levels of financing, respectively, continues to be unstable as a trend. The level of financing of fundamental research has to be determined by considering the needs of other stakeholders who also make a contribution and usually follow a different deadline and priorities.

It is possible to focus the development of programmes on a comprehensive portfolio of studies, rather than on individual short-term programmes or projects, in order to provide flexibility with regards to the changing environment. This could ensure a more long-term focus on multi-disciplinary studies.

In general, it is expected that studies will add value, but the more important question is how exactly they do and how it is measured. Empirical studies confirm the common-sense expectation that members of clusters have higher innovation capacity (Angelov, 2021). The industry has an absorbing capacity for using the outcomes from scientific research, and a significant part of the research organisations directly work with companies in order to demonstrate the results from scientific research and build a capacity for a future transfer of knowledge, instead of immediately realising its potential. However, earlier studies (Bankova & Mihaylova, 2014) identified serious incompetence in cluster management in Bulgaria. The same study recommends actions targeting trust, responsibility, and relationship management with the external environment.

References

Angelov, I. (2021). Level of Innovative capacity of ICT sector organisations according to their participation in industrial cluster. *Strategies for Policy in Science and Education*, 29 (4), 354–369.

Australian Research Council (2009). *ERA Indicator Principles*, https://www.yumpu.com/en/document/view/14822755/era-indicators-consultation-paper-australian-research-council

Ayikoru, M., Tribe, J., & Airey, D. (2009). Reading Tourism Education: Neoliberalism Unveiled. *Annals of Tourism Research*, 36 (2), 191–221. DOI: 10.1016/j.annals.2008.11.001

Bach, L., & Wolff, S. (2017). The BETA-EvaRIO impact evaluation method: towards a bridging approach? *The Journal of Technology Transfer*. DOI: 10.1007/s10961-017-9603-y

Banal-Estañol, A., Jofre-Bonet, M., & Lawson, C. (2015). The double-edged sword of industry collaboration: Evidence from engineering academics in the UK. *Research Policy*, 44 (6), 1160–1175, https://doi.org/10.1016/j.respol.2015.02.006

Bankova, A., & Mihaylova, I. (2014). Clusters, Conflicts, Management. *Yearbook of the Faculty of Economics and Business Administration, Sofia University*, 12 (1), 23–33.

Bastow, S., Dunleavy, P., & Tinkler, J. (2014). *The impact of the social sciences: How academics and their research make a difference*. Los Angeles CA: Sage, https://www.doi.org/10.4135/9781473921511

Belcher, B. M., & Hughes, K. (2021). Understanding and evaluating the impact of integrated problem-oriented research programmes: Concepts and considerations. *Research Evaluation*, 30 (2), 154–168, https://doi.org/10.1093/reseval/rvaa024

Bornmann, L., & Marx, W. (2013). How good is research really? *EMBO Reports*, 14 (3), 226–230, https://doi.org/10.1038/embor.2013.9

Bozeman, B., Fay, D., & Slade, C. P. (2013). Research collaboration in universities and academic entrepreneurship: The-state-of-the-art. *Journal of Technology Transfer*, 38 (1), 1–67, https://doi.org/10.1007/s10961-012-9281-8

Bozeman, B., Gaughan, M., Youtie, J., Slade, C. P., & Rimes, H. (2015). Research collaboration experiences, good and bad: Dispatches from the front lines. *Science and Public Policy*, 43 (2), 226–244, https://doi.org/10.1093/scipol/scv035

Brown, R., & Carasso, H. (2013.) *Everything for sale? The marketisation of UK higher education*. Abingdon: Routledge

Buckland, R. (2009). Private and Public Sector Models for Strategies in Universities. *British Journal of Management*, 20, 524–536, https://doi.org/10.1111/j.1467-8551.2008.00593.x

Cartwright, N. (2003). Two Theorems on Invariance and Causality. *Philosophy of Science*, 70 (1), 203–224, https://doi.org/10.1086/367876

Clarke, C. A., & Knights, D. (2015). Careering through academia: Securing identities or engaging ethical subjectivities? *Human Relations*, 68 (12), 1865–1888, https://doi.org/10.1177/0018726715570978

Coates, J. F. (1971), Technology Assessment: The Benefits ... the Costs ... the Consequences. *The Futurist*, 5 (December), 225–231.

Davies, H., Nutley, S., & Walter, I. (2005) *Assessing the Impact of Social Science Research: Conceptual Methodological and Practical Issues*, https://esrc.ukri.org/files/research/research-and-impact-evaluation/international-symposium/

Donovan, C. (2011). Impact is a Strong Weapon for Making an Evidence-Based Case Study for Enhanced Research Support but a State-of-the-Art Approach to Measurement is Needed. *LSE Blog*, http://eprints.lse.ac.uk/51839/

Donovan, C., & Hanney, S. (2011). The 'Payback Framework' explained, *Research Evaluation*, 20 (3), 181–183, https://doi.org/10.3152/095820211X13118583635756

Duryea, M., Hochman, M., & Parfitt, A. (2007). Measuring the Impact of Research. *Research Global*, 27, 8–9, https://www.guidelines.kaowarsom.be/documents/ResGlob2007.pdf

References

Earl, S., Carden, F., & Smutylo, T. (2001). *Outcome mapping: Building learning and reflection into development programs*. International Development Research Centre, https://media.africaportal.org/documents/Outcome_Mapping_Building_Learning_and_Reflection_into_Development_Programs.pdf

Etzioni, A. (2001). Humble Decision Making. *Harvard Business Review on Decision Making*, 45–57. https://ssrn.com/abstract=2157020

European Commission (2013). *EVALSED: The resource for the evaluation of Socio-Economic Development – Evaluation guide*. European Commission, https://ec.europa.eu/regional_policy/sources/docgener/evaluation/guide/evaluation_sourcebook.pdf

European Commission (2017). *Better Regulation Guidelines*. SWD (2017) 350, https://ec.europa.eu/info/sites/default/files/better-regulation-guidelines.pdf

European Science Foundation (2009). *Evaluation in National Research Funding Agencies: Approaches, Experiences and Case Studies*, https://www.esf.org/fileadmin/user_upload/esf/MO_Evaluation-RFO-Report_2012.pdf

Gaffikin, F., & Perry, D. C. (2009). Discourses and Strategic Visions: The U.S. Research University as an Institutional Manifestation of Neoliberalism in a Global Era. *American Educational Research Journal*, 46 (1), 115–144, https://doi.org/10.3102/0002831208322180

Gordon, Th. (1994) *Cross-Impact Method*, http://www1.ximb.ac.in/users/fac/dpdash/dpdash.nsf/23e5e39594c064ee852564ae004fa010/2a7a6240bcf05ebde5256906000a7322/$file/cross-im.pdf

Grant, J. (2006) *Measuring the Benefits from Research*. RAND Europe, https://www.rand.org/content/dam/rand/pubs/research_briefs/2007/RAND_RB9202.pdf

Gunn, A., & Mintrom, M. (2018). Measuring Research Impact in Australia. *Australian Universities' Review*, 60, 9–15.

Hanney, S. R., & González-Block, M. A. (2011). Yes, research can inform health policy; but can we bridge the 'Do-Knowing It's Been Done' gap? *Health Research Policy and Systems*, 9 (1), 23, https://doi.org/10.1186/1478-4505-9-23

Hemsley-Brown, J., & Oplatka, I. (2006). Universities in a competitive global marketplace: A systematic review of the literature on higher education marketing. *International Journal of Public Sector Management*, 19 (4), 316–338, https://doi.org/10.1108/09513550610669176

Hewitt-Dundas, N. (2012). Research intensity and knowledge transfer activity in UK universities. *Research Policy*, 41 (2), 262–275, https://doi.org/10.1016/j.respol.2011.10.01

Hicks, D. (2012). Performance-based university research funding systems. *Research Policy*, 41 (2), 251–261, https://doi.org/10.1016/j.respol.2011.09.007

Hinrichs-Krapels, S., & Grant, J. (2016). Exploring the effectiveness, efficiency and equity (3e's) of research and research impact assessment. *Palgrave Communications*, 2 (1), 16090, https://doi.org/10.1057/palcomms.2016.90

Hummelbrunner, R. (2006). *Process Monitoring of Impacts: Proposal for a new approach to monitor the implementation of "Territorial Cooperation" programmes*. European Union, https://docplayer.net/20007027-Process-monitoring-of-impacts.html

International Association for Impact Assessment, https://www.iaia.org/index.php

Joly, P.-B., & Matt, M. (2017). Towards a new generation of research impact assessment approaches. *The Journal of Technology Transfer*, https://doi.org/10.1007/s10961-017-9601-0

Kamenetzky, A., & Hinrichs-Krapels, S. (2020) How do organisations implement research impact assessment (RIA) principles and good practice? A narrative review and exploratory study of four international research funding and administrative organisations. *Health Research Policy and Systems*, 18, Article No. 6, https://doi.org/10.1186/s12961-019-0515-1

Kelly, U., & McNicoll, I. (2011). *Through a Glass, Darkly: Measuring the Social Value of Universities*. National Co-ordinating Centre for Public Engagement, https://www.publicengagement.ac.uk/sites/default/files/80096%20NCCPE%20Social%20Value%20Report.pdf

Lašáková, A., Bajzíková, Ľ., & Dedze, I. (2017). Barriers and drivers of innovation in higher education: Case study-based evidence across ten European universities. *International Journal of Educational Development*, 55, 69–79, https://doi.org/10.1016/j.ijedudev.2017.06.002

Marchant, P. (2017). Why lighting claims might be wrong. *International Journal of Sustainable Lighting*, 19, 69–74, https://doi.org/10.26607/ijsl.v19i1.71

Mayne, J. (1999). *Addressing attribution through contribution analysis: using performance measures sensibly*, http://www.oag-bvg.gc.ca/internet/docs/99dp1_e.pdf

Mayne, J. (2001) Addressing attribution through contribution analysis: using performance measures sensibly. *The Canadian Journal of Program Evaluation*, 16 (1), 1–24.

Mayne, J., & The Institutional Learning and Change (ILAC) Initiative (2008). *Contribution analysis: An approach to exploring cause and effect*, https://www.betterevaluation.org/sites/default/files/ILAC_Brief16_Contribution_Analysis.pdf

Naudé, P., & Ivy, J. (1999). The marketing strategies of universities in the United Kingdom. *International Journal of Educational Management*, 13 (3), 126–136. DOI: 10.1108/09513549910269485

Newson, R., King, L., Rychetnik, L., Milat, A., & Bauman, A. (2018). Looking both ways: a review of methods for assessing research impacts on policy and the policy utilisation of research. *Health Research Policy and Systems*, 16 (1), https://doi.org/10.1186/s12961-018-0310-4

Nigohosyan, D., & Vutsova, A. (2018). The 2014–2020 European Regional Development Fund Indicators: The Incomplete Evolution. *Social Indicators Research*, 137, 559–577, https://doi.org/10.1007/s11205-017-1610-8

OECD Committee on Science and Technology Policy / OECD Working Party on Innovation and Technology Policy (TIP) (2009). *Enhancing Public Research Performance through Evaluation, Impact Assessment and Priority Setting*, https://www.oecd.org/sti/inno/Enhancing-Public-Research-Performance.pdf

Orr, L. (1997). Globalisation and universities: Towards the "market university"? *Social Dynamics*, 23 (1), 42–67. DOI: 10.1080/02533959708458619

Penfield, T., Baker, M. J., Scoble, R., & Wykes, M. C. (2014). Assessment, evaluations, and definitions of research impact: A review. *Research Evaluation*. DOI: 10.1093/reseval/rvt021

Porter, A. L., & Rossini, F. A. (2019). *Why Integrated Impact Assessment?*, https://doi.org/10.4324/9780429045196-1

Ragin, C. C., & Sonnett, J. (2005). *Between Complexity and Parsimony: Limited Diversity, Counterfactual Cases, and Comparative Analysis*, https://doi.org/10.1007/978-3-322-80441-9_9

Rollins, L, Llewellyn, N, Ngaiza, M, Nehl, E, Carter, D. R., & Sands, J. M. Using the payback framework to evaluate the outcomes of pilot projects supported by the Georgia Clinical and Translational Science Alliance. *Journal of Clinical and Translational Science*, 5 (48), 1–9. DOI: 10.1017/cts.2020.542

Seus, S., & Bührer, S. (2017). The evaluation of the Austrian START programme: an impact analysis of a research funding programme using a multi-method approach. *The Journal of Technology Transfer*. DOI: 10.1007/s10961-017-9606-8

Sharpe, A., & Smith, J. (2005). Measuring the Impact of Research on Well-being: A Survey of Indicators of Well-being. *CSLS Research Reports*, https://www.semanticscholar.org/paper/Measuring-the-Impact-of-Research-on-Well-being%3A-A-Sharpe-Smith/d2a0754f1332002f8fd0e1cd97f919d0ba21e135

Sorde, T. (2015, May). *SIOR: recognition of the social impact of research through open science resources* [Conference presentation]. ORCID and Casrai joint conference, Barcelona, Spain, https://www.slideshare.net/ORCIDSlides/sorde-teresa

Spaapen, J., & Drooge, L. (2011). Introducing 'Productive Interactions' in Social Impact Assessment. *Research Evaluation*, 20 (3), 211–218. DOI: 10.3152/095820211X12941371876742

Spaapen, J., van Drooge, L., Propp, T., van der Meulen, B., Shinn, T., Marcovich, A., van den Besselaar, P., Jong, S., Barker, K., Cox, D., Morrison, K., Sveinsdottir, T. Pearson, D., D'Oppolitto, B., Prins, A., Molas, J., Tang, P., & Castro-Martínez, E. (2011). *SIAMPI final report. Social Impact Assessment Methods for research and funding instruments through the study of Productive Interactions between science and society*. The University of Sheffield, Research Services, https://www.sheffield.ac.uk/rs/impact/pathways

Thomas, R. (2018). *Questioning the Assessment of Research Impact: Illusions, Myths and Marginal Sectors*. Palgrave Pivot, Cham, https://doi.org/10.1007/978-3-319-95723-4

Thomas, R., & Ormerod, N. (2017). The (almost) imperceptible impact of tourism research on policy and practice. *Tourism Management*, 62, 379–389.

Tran, T. A., & Daim, T. (2008). A taxonomic review of methods and tools applied in technology assessment. *Technological Forecasting and Social Change*, 75 (9), 1396–1405, https://doi.org/10.1016/j.techfore.2008.04.004

Vonortas, N., & Link, A. (2013). *Handbook on the Theory and Practice of Program Evaluation*. Cheltenham UK: Edward Elgar.

Watermeyer, R. (2016). Impact in the REF: Issues and obstacles. *Studies on Higher Education*, 41 (2), 199–214, https://doi.org/10.1080/03075079.2014.915303

Wooding, S., Nason, E., Klautzer, L., Rubin, J., Hanney, S., & Grant, J. (2007). *Policy and practice impacts of research funded by the Economic and Social Research Council: A case study of the Future of Work programme, approach and analysis*, Santa Monica CA: RAND Corporation, https://www.rand.org/pubs/technical_reports/TR435.html

Yudkevich, M., Altbach, P. G., & Rumbley, L. E. (2016). *The global academic rankings game: Changing institutional policy, practice and academic life*. Abingdon: Routledge, https://www.routledge.com/The-Global-Academic-Rankings-Game-Changing-Institutional-Policy-Practice/Yudkevich-Altbach-Rumbley/p/book/9781138935792

III. Main Methodologies

The approaches to the assessment differ significantly due to the political orientation of the relevant organisation (its mission and objectives), the institutional environment, and the nature of the subjects which are under examination (higher education institutions and their substructures, horizontal research organisations, target programmes, etc.) The national assessment of studies may lead to an institutional change, and so the evaluating institutions and teams will be able to adapt their actions and will better address the expectations of their users.

We are trying to determine to what extent the research assessment methods can stimulate the development of research assessment itself and whether they are formalised and directly influence the innovation ecosystem. This study investigates whether and how the assessment of research activity or elements thereof influence the research environment or parts of it for a particular period of time. The following research questions are posed:

- Which is the most preferred assessment system on a national level and which assessment system is universally applicable?
- What determines the differences in preference (choices) with regards to introducing the assessment system in different countries?
- Is there an intervention in the research environment as a result of the performance of a research assessment and how is that intervention made?
- Does transformation in the research environment occur as a result of the research assessment and, if yes, can we determine the sectors (fields) where the impact is the strongest?

We study the possibility for a dynamic in the research efficiency and, respectively, the possibilities for a re-programming of the national research environment. A review of the research assessment practices which use a combination of different indicators was performed, and a comparative analysis based on several European assessment systems was prepared.

In searching of excellent research evaluation system one should look everywhere, of course. This includes western (presumably as a source of good practice) and eastern European countries (as a mirroring exercise to see how others in a similar situation coped with the challenges of transforming the higher education and research systems).

Through the Scholarnet project we institutionally tried to learn from the French (UVSQ/Paris Saclay) and the German systems (FAU Erlangen Nuremberg). In both countries (tenure) professors are mainly public servants, which is quite different from the situation in Bulgaria and other transition countries. Eastern European countries tend to favour academic inbreeding and even base their proud on this pattern (for instance the Sofia Logics School or the Bulgarian school of medieval philosophy). The German system fosters diversity by getting degrees from different universities and ending up as a tenure professor elsewhere, or at least after a considerably long period in one of your alma maters.

Austria had transformed its system of hiring professors at public universities away from the civil servants system (since 2004) and Netherlands was running its universities more or less in a "private" way. Institutionally the host institution of the authors had close cooperation with German universities such as the University of Cologne, FAU Erlangen Nuremberg, Humboldt University and others, we looked at its system, but found it institutionally distant from the Eastern Europe. The way "schools of thought" emerge in German universities is by having a relatively longer "pre-tenure career" – PhD projects take longer than in Eastern Europe and also "chairs" in universities could hire a lot of fixed-term assistants. In Bulgaria, for instance you can get a tenure position at assistant professor level just after the PhD defence and for quite long time you could have retired as an assistant professor without a PhD. The accreditation systems of universities and programs provide incentives or even require to have significantly larger share of tenured lecturers (unlimited labour contract). As a rule, you should have 70 % of all courses thought by "internal" lecturers (on unlimited contracts).

The German accreditation system, unlike most of the Eastern European countries, is organized in a decentralized way and is characterized by its two approaches to accreditation. On the one hand the accreditation of degree programmes (programme accreditation) and on the other the accreditation of the quality assurance system within a university (system accreditation), both conducted by accreditation agencies which need authorisation from the Accreditation Council (accreditation of agencies).

The Accreditation Council as a central decision-making body defines fundamental requirements for the accreditation of study programmes, the accreditation of quality assurance systems and the accreditation agencies.

In addition, it is responsible for reliable, transparent and internationally accepted criteria as a basis for all of the above accreditations

The programme and system accreditation procedures are characterised by a two-stage procedure: The assessment and preparation of an accreditation report with recommendations for resolutions and assessments in accordance with the standards laid down in the Specimen decree is organised by an agency commissioned by the higher education institution. The responsibility for the accreditation decision, however, lies with the Accreditation Council. At the request of the higher education institution, the Accreditation Council decides on the accreditation of a study programme or the internal quality management system of the higher education institution. The decision is made on the basis of the accreditation report, whereby a justified deviation from the expert recommendation is possible.

The applicable criteria for research assessment as a part of general accreditation include individual achievements in teaching, writing proposals or publications adequately recognised. Performance evaluation is not limited to merely counting the number of publications or comparing index factors.

Performance evaluation should primarily be based on qualitative standards. Assessment of the achievement of a researchers must be carried out in its entirety and based on substantive qualitative criteria. In addition to the publication of articles, books, data and software, other dimensions can be taken into account, such as involvement in teaching, academic self-administration, public relations or knowledge and technology transfer. Details of quantitative metrics such as impact factors and h-indices are not required and are not to be considered as part of the review. Accreditation focuses on curricula (assessed for quality), research is not an explicit object of this assessment, although present as a criterion.

The collaboration with the German scientific societies is of prime importance for all the countries in the focus of this research. Germany is the preferred partner for new member states. The ongoing intensive networking gives access to circulation of good practices, higher potential of the research and better performance.

The study is based on the analysis of information about research in the following European countries: Austria, Bulgaria, Lithuania, the Netherlands, Poland, Slovenia, Hungary and the Czech Republic. Different data were extracted from legal documents and from the official websites of the institutions which curate the policies and the performance of research in the country (ministries and agencies). The various public financing flows in

III. Main Methodologies

the countries, subject of the study, were identified. The individual criteria applied for the purpose of research assessment, and their grouping or accompanying weights, if any, were examined in detail. This analysis served as a basis for outlining the most common types of indicators used in the performance of research assessment. A preference was observed with regards to the application of different types of criteria which is due to variations both in terms of the duration of assessment procedures, and the organisational and institutional culture of the individual countries. Thanks to various analytical and research activities, all countries adopt actions aiming to exclude conditions for conflicts of interests in research evaluation processes.

Indicators characterising the condition of the national innovation ecosystems were used to study the influence of research assessment. The respective data were extracted from the reports published by Innovation Scoreboard since 2010 and Eurostat; also data provided by the European Commission with regards to the participation of Member States in the Horizon 2020 programme were used.

This was fine-tuned using the expertise of one of the authors (Albena Vutsova), a long-standing manager of the Scientific Research Fund, Head of the Science Directorate in the Ministry of Education and Science, and professor at Sofia University St. Kliment Ohridski. Within the last 15 to 20 years, almost all criteria systems for assessment of research projects and programmes on a national level were developed, and the best practices of most Member States were reported. The common approach to these activities is grounded in science-based methodology.

The methodology combined the author's own elaborations and experience gained during the performance of periodic research assessments of European structures such as the Joint Research Centre (JCR) and periodic assessments of science and innovation framework programmes of the Community with the implementation of formal methods such as interviews, surveys, and an analysis of a series of relevant documents which are necessary for the assessment.

Consultations with national and foreign experts were carried out with regards to some of the interpretations (including 10 interviews with stakeholders, such as representatives of specialised directorates at the relevant ministries and agencies, university rectors, the chairman of the Council of Rectors, deputy chairmen of the Bulgarian Academy of Sciences and the National Centre for Agrarian Science, and ad hoc assessment work groups at JCR). The analysis of the national research assessment system was evalu-

III. Main Methodologies

ated and verified within the COST Action 15137 European programme where part of the results were incorporated in the national research assessment report. In-depth interviews with over 50 participants who are part of the assessment process were organised. The interviews were conversation-based, the respondents also had to complete questionnaires. Thirty-five respondents were asked to provide written answers; the survey included 20 questions, of which 30 % were open-ended.

In addition, a number of documents were analysed in the work process:

- ex-ante evaluation of Operational Programme 'Science and Education for Smart Growth', Bulgaria[5];
- ex-ante evaluation of the Innovations Programme, Hungary[6];
- organisational evaluation of the Hungarian Scientific Research Fund (OTKA)[7];
- analyses of the Horizon Policy Support Facility (PSF) of the European Commission for Bulgaria (Peer Review of the Bulgarian Research and Innovation system)[8];
- analyses of the Horizon Policy Support Facility (PSF) of the European Commission for Hungary (Peer Review of the Hungarian Research and Innovation system)[9];
- analyses of the Horizon Policy Support Facility (PSF) of the European Commission for Poland (Peer Review of Poland's Higher Education and Science System)[10];
- two reports on the assessment of the implementation of the most recently completed framework programmes (7 Framework Programme and Horizon 2020 – interim)[11];

---

5 http://www.opnoir.bg/?go=page&pageId=55&lang=en
6 https://www.fi-compass.eu/sites/default/files/publications/Ex-Ante_GAP_TO12348_vegso_EN.pdf
7 https://www.esf.org/fileadmin/user_upload/esf/OTKA_Evaluation-Report_final2014 1104.pdf
8 https://ec.europa.eu/research-and-innovation/sites/default/files/rio/report/Full%2520report%2520-%2520Peer% 2520Review%2520of%2520the%2520BG%2520RI%2520system%2520under%2520the%2520PSF.pdf
9 https://ec.europa.eu/research-and-innovation/sites/default/files/rio/report/H2020PSF%2520peer%2520review% 2520report% 2520Hungary-KI0216982ENNHU.pdf
10 https://ec.europa.eu/research-and-innovation/sites/default/files/rio/report/PSF-Peer_review_Poland__FINAL%2520REPORT.pdf
11 https://op.europa.eu/en/publication-detail/-/publication/7e74df87-ebb0-11e8-b690-01aa75ed71a1/language-en/format-PDF/source-80689114; https://op.europa.eu/en/pu

- evaluation of the research programme of the Joint Research Centre (JCR) – EC[12];
- reports of the Joint Research Centre (JCR) – EC[13];
- proceedings (collections of publications) from international research conferences dedicated to issues relating to research assessment[14];
- scholarly articles dedicated to research assessment systems penned by experts in the field;
- peer review organised under the INTERREG EUROPE 2014–2020 (internal report);
- legal documents with a focus on the research system in individual countries and on strategies for smart specialisation and development of research and innovation;
- guidelines for conducting a research assessment;
- reports of the national ministries and agencies for research and innovation;
- OECD documents with a focus on analysis of the research and educational system in the countries examined;
- publications on research systems in Eurydice;
- annual reports of the ranking system for higher education institutions in Bulgaria;
- over 30 individual e-mail communications with stakeholders from different organisations and communication via ordinary means.

The expert evaluation of the team with regards to the effects of research assessment on the innovation ecosystem was validated through discussions with international experts (lecturers and researchers at the University of Lausanne, University of Porto, University of Twente, Sofia University "St. Kliment Ohridski", Vilnius University, University of Lisbon, etc.) who study similar issues and participate in relevant EU projects. Part of the conclusions is featured in an internal summary report on the research assessment practices of Member States and EU membership candidate countries.

The study is limited to countries which have, to a certain extent, a similar demographic and socio-economic profile. On the other hand, it was taken

---

blication-detail/-/publication/fad8c173-7e42-11e7-b5c6-01aa75ed71a1/language-en/format-PDF/source-77918455

12 https://publications.jrc.ec.europa.eu/repository/handle/JRC96870
13 https://ideas.repec.org/p/ipt/iptwpa/jrc101136.html
14 https://scholarlypublications.universiteitleiden.nl/search?type=dismax&f%5B0%5D=mods_relatedItem_host_titleInfo_title_ms%3ASTI%5C%202018%5C%20Conference%5C%20Proceedings; http://informationr.net/ir/22-1/colis/colis1623.html

into account that there is a lack of standardised and fully comparable indicators and detailed data about the weight of the criteria.

There are no universal methodologies which will meet all needs and requirements with regards to the performance of a research assessment. Each methodology is defined by the objectives and functions of the specific research organisations. According to Gonda and Kakizaki (1995), the methods for assessing policies, programmes, and the quality of the research vary significantly. When the assessments relate to a large-scale programme, oriented towards a mission of the relevant organisation, it is more suitable to conduct a cost-benefit analysis. With regards to target programmes, accompanied by dissemination of results, it is recommended to conduct a more specific analysis which requires precise quantitative and qualitative data. Programmes targeted at raising awareness or public consultations require feedback from users, which is significant.

The various assessment methods have originated and been developed depending on the stages of the research and technological development of a given country. Methods evaluating the quality of research, which is measured through peer review and/or bibliometrics, are more frequently used. This approach requires quantity-oriented techniques.

Over the course of time, the assessment process has undergone transformation and has adopted the approach based on a portfolio of criteria. An in-depth assessment requires the application of both qualitative and quantitative methods which complement each other. That is why the implementation of alternative methods leads to more credible results and realistic recommendations (Hong & Boden, 2003). Hong and Boden (2003) conduct an in-depth study of the R&D assessment and comment on both the theoretical and practical aspects. They provide an overview of the various systems and types of assessment.

Kostoff (1993) differentiates the individual types of assessments with regards to quality and quantity. The following may be indicated as qualitative assessments: presence of strategic documents, positioning on an international level, etc.; quantitative assessments include bibliometrics, cost-benefit analysis, etc.

Hafkesbrink and Krause (1995) propose a technological method for assessing the economic aspect of technologies. Hong and Boden (2003) consider it an invaluable instrument in the assessment of research and development and innovation processes and believe that it could be implemented in both fundamental and applied studies.

III. Main Methodologies

Georghiou (1999) also suggests an alternative categorisation of the assessment methods. One such method is an assessment framework: the comparison of the situation before/after the assessment, control group, and a counterfactual and logical analysis. Interviews, statistical data, and a review of different strategic documents are also used in some of these methods.

The research assessment methodology applied in Bulgaria uses a mix of different approaches. In order to outline to what extent this methodology is relevant and provides the necessary intervention in the ecosystem, detailed interviews were conducted with Bulgarian scholars working in the academic environment (the total number of scholars is 13,410 – last update: 28/02/2022 according to data provided by the National Statistics Institute[15]) and with administrators involved in the implementation of this sectoral policy.

According to the respondents, the most preferred assessment method is the one based on expertise, which is considered as the most suitable method for the research system in Bulgaria. On the other hand, the systems which have very similar evaluation criteria are the target-oriented assessment and the user-oriented assessment. The former is also referred to as deconstructed assessment, which focuses on specific aspects of the subject of assessment, where a comparison based on standard indicators is recommended in order to see whether an improvement is needed and what measures have to be implemented and for how long. In the latter, the user-oriented assessment, clients form their perceptions based on the technical performance of the service, including functional, mechanical, and human qualities. The third method, the competition-oriented, received significantly lower support by the respondents. This result indirectly confirms the proposition that due to the lower share of financial support, based on direct or indirect competitive principle, there is no definitive agreement that research assessment, especially on an institutional level, should be competition-oriented.

---

15 https://nsi.bg/en/content/2692/researchers-age-and-sex-government-sector-and-higher-education-sector

III. Main Methodologies

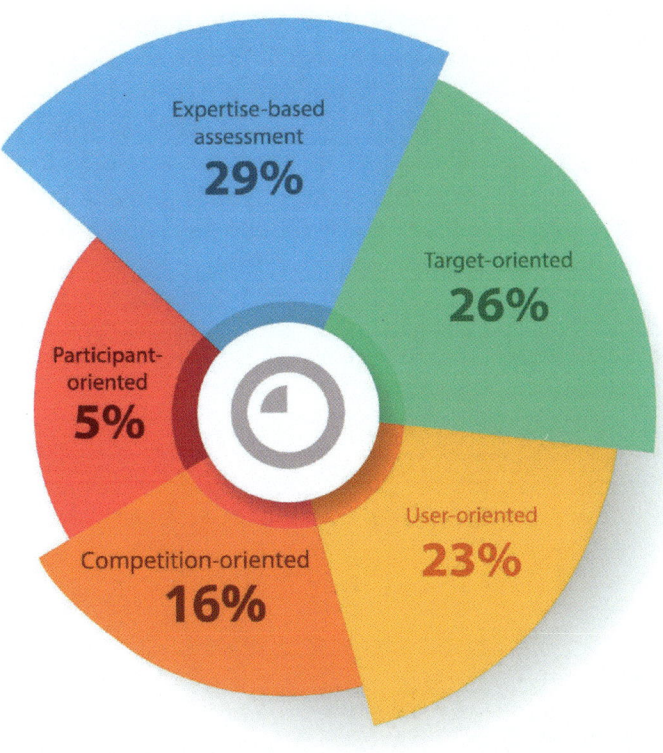

Source: Authors' own elaboration.

Figure 3.1: Preferred research assessment category in Bulgaria

The institutional-pluralistic assessment (which is focused mainly on communicating economic sustainability) gains only a slight majority of the votes; one explanation may be that for many respondents research assessment is mainly useful to the policy-making institutions and contributes primarily to re-designing the research policy. This, of course, suggests that a number of economic factors (return on investment, IPR, optimisation of market realisation) should be taken into account in order to achieve a significant change in the research policy. On the other hand, the institutional

III. Main Methodologies

approach entails an adherence to formal and informal rules, procedures, norms, etc. In this context, the academia demonstrates a preference for the institutional-pluralistic assessment. Many respondents still assume the evaluation process as a possible policy adjustment, rather than as a means of assessing the effectiveness of a given research as a basis for improving the eco-innovation media. In addition, the respondents' opinion with regards to the degree of intervention in the research system through assessment shows that there is a visible intervention in the system, but it is far away from achieving a sustainable change in the innovation ecosystem. Large share of the respondents believe that the benefit of research assessment is mainly a conceptual one, which is in unison with the finding regarding its use to policy-making organisations.

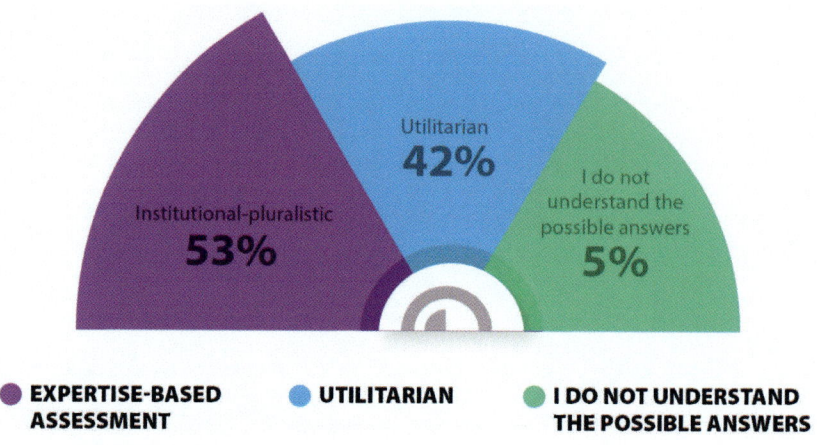

Source: Authors' own elaboration.

Figure 3.2: Preferred alternative assessment

The study shows that the assessment of individual aspects of the research system in Bulgaria applies the summative type of assessment (one which summarises the results achieved so far and indicates the shortcomings). This is natural in the context of the set of assessment criteria, which appear to be not very well synchronised in specific cases. However, there is an ambition to reflect the specificities of the system in a more efficient way.

The type of assessment approach to be employed (summative or formative) largely depends on the subject of evaluation. For individual items (for example, project, researcher, period), it is more suitable to implement the formative type of assessment (which takes the longest as it is conducted during the entire process and provides information about the work efficiency), while for group subjects (including teams, systems, and organisations) it is more appropriate to implement the summative type of assessment.

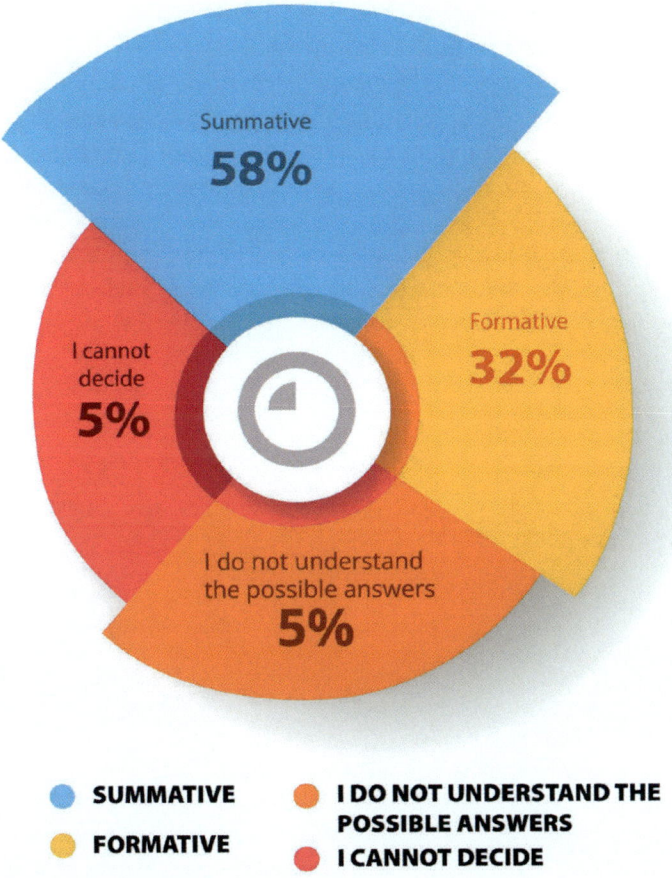

Source: Authors' own elaboration.

Figure 3.3: *Type of assessment with regards to individual aspects of the research system*

The study also analyses the extent to which the inclusion of stakeholders in the process of research assessment or the initiation of this process influences the impact and transformation of the entire innovation ecosystem.

III. Main Methodologies

The results confirm that the stakeholders' views are considered; we therefore conclude that research assessment will have an effect on the entire ecosystem or individual system elements. The level of impact will depend on the institutional weight of the respective stakeholders.

An interesting result from the study concerns the implementation of the principles of responsive assessment (that is, the ratio between a set of values, which a given research activity would propose, and a set of expectations and criteria, which different participants have for this activity). Respondents believe that this principle is generally not implemented, and wherever it is implemented, this is done on rare occasions and/or partially.

This finding is surprising, considering the overall perception of education and science as a public good; prosperity, apparently, this public good fails to meet society's expectations. In terms of valorisation, respondents reported that some studies produce value both for academia and for society, yet a big part of this value is not quantifiable; at the same time the action itself is subject to a lot of responsibilities (collegial/professional).

III. Main Methodologies

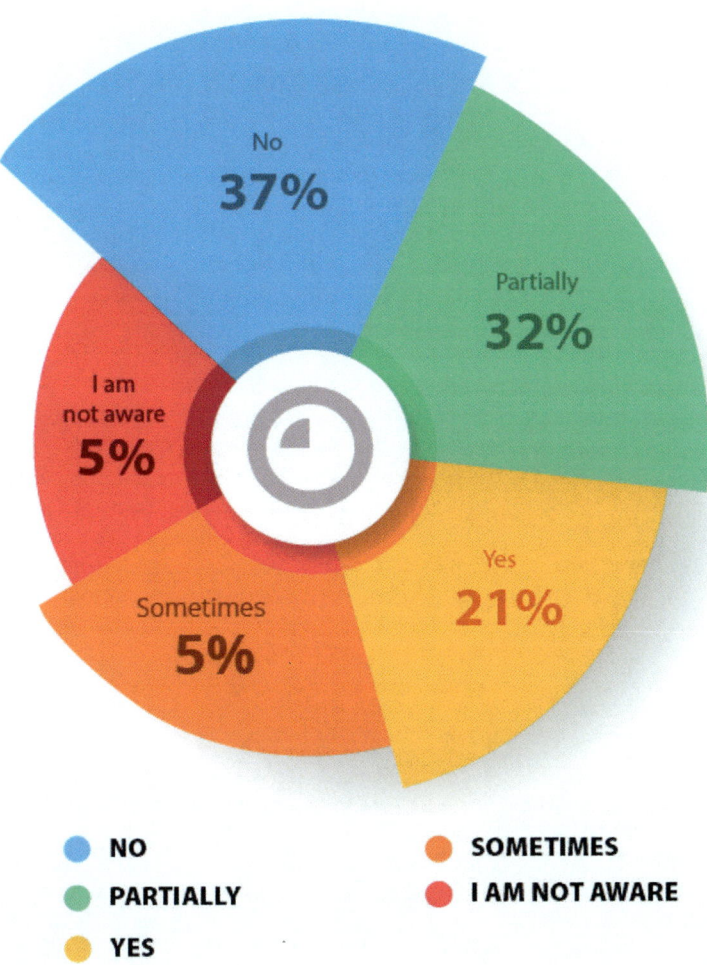

Source: Authors' own elaboration.

Figure 3.4: Implementation of a set of values, expectations, and criteria

The next chapter presents and compares different approaches to research assessment in the European countries listed above in order to find an answer to the research questions posed. Particular attention is paid to the types of criteria applied in research assessment and their comparison.

References

Bach, L., Conde-Molist, N., Ledoux, M. J., Matt, M., & Schaeffer, V. (1995). Evaluation of the economic effects of Brite-Euram programmes on the European industry. *Scientometrics*, 34, 325–349, https://doi.org/10.1007/BF02018003

Ecorys South East Europe Ltd. (2014). *Ex-ante Evaluation of Operational Programme Science and Education for Smart Growth 2014–2020*. Ministry of Science and Education, Bulgaria, http://www.opnoir.bg/?go=page&pageId=55&lang=en

European Commission (1997). *Evaluation of the Brite-Euram: A Decade of Developing Competitiveness*, http://aei.pitt.edu/44939/1/A7266.pdf

European Commission., Directorate-General for Research and Innovation (2015a). *Peer review of the Bulgarian research and innovation system. Horizon 2020 policy support facility*. European Commission. DOI: 10.2777/17938

European Commission., Directorate-General for Research and Innovation. (2015b). *Commitment and Coherence – Ex-Post Evaluation of the 7th EU Framework Programme*. European Commission, https://op.europa.eu/en/publication-detail/-/publication/7e74df87-ebb0-11e8-b690-01aa75ed71a1/language-en/format-PDF/source-80689114

European Commission., Directorate-General for Research and Innovation. (2016). *Peer Review of the Hungarian Research and Innovation system*. Publications Office of the European Union. DOI: 10.2777/236994

European Commission., Directorate-General for Research and Innovation. (2017a). *Interim evaluation of Horizon 2020*. European Commission, https://op.europa.eu/en/publication-detail/-/publication/fad8c173-7e42-11e7-b5c6-01aa75ed71a1/language-en/format-PDF/source-77918455

European Commission., Directorate-General for Research and Innovation. (2017b). *Peer Review of Poland's Higher Education and Science System*. Publications Office of the European Union. DOI: 0.2777/193011

Georghiou, L. (1999). Socio-Economic Effects of Collaborative R&D-European Experiences. *Journal of Technology Transfer*, 24, 69–79, https://doi.org/10.1023/A:1007724804288

Gonda, K., & Kakizaki, F. (1995). Research, Technology and Development Evaluation; Developments in Japan. *Scientometrics*, 34 (3), 375–389, https://doi.org/10.1007/BF02018006

Guba, E. G., & Lincoln, Y. S. (1989). *Fourth Generation Evaluation*. London: Sage, https://doi.org/10.1007/bf02018006

Haegeman, K., Spiesberger, M., & Konnola, T. (2014). *Evaluating foresight in transnational research programming*. Paper presented at FTA conference 2014 (Future-oriented Technology Analysis). Brussels, https://www.zsi.at/de/object/publication/3679

Joint Research Centre (2015). *Ex-post Evaluation of the direct actions of the Joint Research Centre under the Seventh Framework Programmes 2007–2013*. European Commission, https://publications.jrc.ec.europa.eu/repository/handle/JRC96870; https://ec.europa.eu/jrc/sites/default/files/ex-post-evaluation-2007-2013_en.pdf

Kostoff, R. (1993). Evaluating Federal R&D in the US. In: B. Boseman & J. Melkers (eds). *Evaluating R&D impacts: Methods and Practice*. Boston: Kluwer Academic Publishers, 79–98.

Kratky, C., Djurhuus, J. C., Hegarty, F., Horvat, M., Realo, A., van der Meulen, B., Boman, J., Phillips, S., & Heywood-Roos, R. (2014). *Organisational Evaluation of the Hungarian Scientific Research Fund) (OTKA) Evaluation Report*. European Science Foundation, https://www.esf.org/fileadmin/user_upload/esf/OTKA_Evaluation-Report_final20141104.pdf

Szazadveg Foundation (2018). *Ex-ante assessment: Phase 1. Hungarian Government*. European Union, https://www.fi-compass.eu/sites/default/files/publications/Ex-Ante_GAP_TO12348_vegso_EN.pdf

Todorova, A., & Slavcheva, M. (2016). *RIO Country Report 2015: Bulgaria*. JRC Working Papers JRC101136, Joint Research Centre (Seville site), https://ideas.repec.org/p/ipt/iptwpa/jrc101136.html

Vutsova, A., Hristov, T., & Arabadzhieva, M. (2019). *Impact Assessment of Research Evaluation: The Bulgarian Case*. CfP: RESSH 2019 – The Third Research Evaluation in the SSH Conference, Valencia, https://enressh.eu/wp-content/uploads/2020/04/ressh2019_book.pdf

Worthen, B. R., Sanders, J. R., & Fitzpatrick, J. L. (1997). *Program Evaluation – Alternative Approaches and Practical Guidelines*. New York: Longman.

IV. Comparing research assessment models on a national level

This chapter presents a comparison of different approaches to the performance of research assessment on a national level in eight selected EU Member States (six 'new' and two 'old' ones), which are relatively similar in geographical, historical, and demographical respect but differ in terms of their innovation performance: Bulgaria, Poland, and Hungary are emerging innovators, the Czech Republic, Slovenia, and Lithuania are moderate innovators, while Netherlands and Austria are strong innovators (European Innovation Scoreboard 2021)[16].

The review of the national practices established that the research assessment and performance-based research funding systems are, in most cases, perceived as part of the political agenda of the country. This activity provides all participants in the national innovation ecosystem with strategic information and allows policy-making institutions to gain a better understanding which is needed to improve the formation of a research development framework and for initiating structural changes.

The effect achieved from the implementation of the research assessment system has to be monitored and evaluated in order to ensure the sustainability of the chosen political strategy and to meet the public needs. Equally important is to provide accountability for the public financial investments that have contributed to this effect.

Various methods are applied for the purpose of conducting research assessment. Researchers in Bulgaria tend to prefer expert evaluation compared to other approaches. Many of the current performance-based research funding systems rely on the analysis of different indicators as an alternative to the expert evaluation method. On the other hand, there is a tendency towards allocating a small part of the research funds according to defined indicators, and the imperfections resulting from this approach are not that significant. 'The informed expert evaluation', where experts use the best indicators available, coupled with other specific information, presents 'the best of both worlds'; this is also an opportunity to make a comparison between an indicator-based and a results-based assessment. To

---

16 https://ec.europa.eu/commission/presscorner/detail/en/IP_21_3048

a certain extent this allows for 'triangulation' between the methods (Arnold & Mahieu, 2015).

In the performance of research assessment significant efforts are devoted to finding a balance between the different types of indicators in the individual research fields or a reasonable explanation as to why there are such differences. Systems that rely on expert evaluation use mechanisms which apply rating scales with equal importance, regardless of the discipline. In the metrics-based approaches, the person responsible for the design/preparation of the assessment has to create a bibliometric technique for the comparison of individual disciplines, and the principals often do not request an in-depth knowledge of their specifics. As a whole, it is easy to design a bibliometric technique which objectivises the subjective expert evaluation, but that is often avoided for political reasons. It is difficult to manipulate an impartial bibliometric technique, and even if it can be manipulated, the unethical practices can be easily identified via algorithms.

The most common type of financial support which research organisations receive is in the form of block grants and performance-based funding. The results-based contracts concluded between the research organisation and the funding organisation are very common, and in some cases they are implemented in combination with specific indicators. They are an important communication tool between research organisations and the policy-making and policy-funding institutions in the field (ministries, agencies). Performance-based systems, on the other hand, are essentially a political instrument and can be altered in order to reach a range of different strategic objectives, which determine the focus and scope of the assessment, its type (summative or formative), the selection of criteria, and the indicators.

An assessment methodology and a funding system function well when they respond to public needs, when public bodies and public policies are well-coordinated, and when there are reliable data and, respectively, reliable sources of information (Arnold & Mahieu, 2015).

1. Is there a common European model?

Research institutions in Europe are facing a number of challenges arising from the dynamic and constantly changing economic and public environment. That is why institutions need to adapt and change/transform the traditional ways of academic work. In this context, a number of issues arise in the performance of research assessment. According to a report by

Science Europe (2020), the European association representing the interests of big public organisations which conduct and fund scientific research, the transparency of the process is an extremely sensitive element in research assessment practices. Ongoing debates focus on the usefulness and application of quantitative indicators, ethical norms in the introduction of the 'open science' paradigm, etc.

The quality of research is perceived subjectively, depending on the specific context; that perception also evolves in time. The lack of a universal definition of research quality and the perception thereof has an effect on transparency. According to a 2019 study, 62 % of the researchers who participated in the survey cannot give a formal definition of quality; only 13 % of the big organisations give a definition of quality, but 38 % of medium-sized organisations and 53 % of the small organisations provide such a definition (Science Europe, 2020). Some institutions report that their assessment criteria are used for the purpose of defining quality, while others say that the definition of the quality of research is determined by the assessors conducting the assessment process. In the assessment criteria of organisations which reported using the term 'excellence' there is a lack of an official and/or universally accepted definition of the term.

The variations in the understanding of quality and which publications shall 'count' as research lead to markedly different behaviours in publication activity. The average number of publications at universities and countries where publishing in top journals is valued and where only those publications are important for academic growth is very small compared to the ones where there is a lack of an independent quality assessment and where quantity is prioritised.

Specific preferences were established in the performance of research assessment. The ones which are most frequently identified have to do with gender (82 %) and discipline (77 %). Others are related to specificities such as belonging (62 %) or position (49 %). Ethnicity is viewed as relevant by only 31 %, whilst 25 % of the organisations participating in the survey look at various types of disabilities.

The lack of cultural diversity among reviewers who conduct the assessment is noted by most organisations (68 %), whilst 32 % of them indicate that there is a need for a more active recruitment of candidates from groups with poor representation. It will be a good idea to acknowledge this finding by creating a portfolio of assessors who are representatives of different cultural communities in order to have conclusions which represent alternative points of view. This will ensure that the assessment is realistic enough while also presenting specific details of the product subject of the assessment.

The same study also examines the 'stability' of the assessment process which is understood as the capacity for choosing processes for a reliable and fair quality assessment of the project proposals. A total of 72 % of the organisations-respondents have looked at the issue of stability of their assessment processes, and 44 % consider it present, whilst 28 % of the respondents have never evaluated the research assessment processes.

Due to the fact that different methods of introduction and popularisation of qualitative indicators in research assessment are used, qualitative review practices are often mixed with quantitative instruments; in particular cases a qualitative-turned-quantitative (through a scoring system) assessment is used and/or an entirely qualitative assessment is applied (Science Europe, 2020).

The research assessment processes and the variety of approaches to its performance are complicated, but regardless of that a number of research organisations share common evaluation practices in their desire to attract quality researchers.

The evaluation system, however, is under ever bigger pressure, and institutions face a number of issues in their attempts to conduct an efficient research assessment. That is why there is a need for changes in this process and for coordinated policies at national level.

The European Universities Association (EUA) believes that the review of research assessment procedures is a shared responsibility, and a coordinated approach is required for that purpose – one which brings together the main participants. Researchers, universities and other research organisations, funding institutions, and politicians have to work together in order to develop more accurate, transparent, and responsible assessment approaches (Saenen & Borrell-Damián, 2019).

2. The Anglo-Saxon research assessment model

As far as the Bulgarian national research assessment policy is influenced, to a certain extent, by the Anglo-Saxon model, we will first look at the specificities of this model before discussing other European practices. It is prevalent in the United Kingdom, and, regardless of the fact that Great Britain is no longer part of the EU, up until recently this model was part of the palette of European practices. The definitions, criteria, and work methods used by the Research Assessment Exercise (RAE) and the Research Excellence Framework (REF) as of 2014 have evolved with each assessment cycle, but the founding principle has always been that public (state) funding has to be based on particular standards which take into account the quality and volume of studies, and the number of researchers who are considered 'active in terms of conducting research'. Three pillars of scientific research are analysed and respectively assessed: bibliometric and scientometric results from studies (i.e., books, articles, patents, software, performances, or any other form of scientific product), the quality of the research environment (infrastructure, policies targeted at support and research development), and prestige indicators (elements which prove the recognition of researchers in the academia and beyond). These common criteria are interpreted or developed from the point of view of individual disciplines and evaluated by different panels, which prepare their own framework documents also known as Panel Criteria or Work Methods (Détourbe, 2016).

According to Johnston (2008), the research assessment practice in the United Kingdom is an excellent example of an institutionalised process with a high impact not only on a researcher's individual career but also on the financial and intellectual status of a group of researchers (especially academic departments) and sometimes of entire universities and other institutions.

While the impact of research assessment varies, there is a visible trend relating to its effect on researchers. In particular cases a negative assessment which is not in line with the criteria set by REA has led to the discharge of research staff (Lucas, 2016). At the same time, researchers are encouraged to seek international recognition, for example, to become members of the boards of journals in different countries, to be invited as guest professors in foreign universities, to be evaluators in foreign research funds, etc. Even though this ambition may seem positive in general, some authors remark that there can be negative consequences, for example, a specialisation which is too narrow, a presentation of manuscripts only in international journals, or an increasing interest in external funding. This has forced some researchers to transfer to fields in which they do not traditionally work and to search funds outside their institution. An orientation towards applied research or commercial activities is observed at the expense of fundamental research even in the field of social sciences and humanities (blue skies research) (Lucas, 2016).

The Research Excellence Framework (REF) entered into force in 2014, and though it is a lot more different than RAE, it does build on the past practice to a certain extent. The main mission of REF is 'to provide accountability for public investment in research and produce evidence for the benefits of this investment' (https://www.ref.ac.uk/). There is no longer just talk about public funding of scientific research, but it suggests an opportunity for a return on investment by introducing a new criterion: the 'impact of scientific research' (Lucas, 2016). In this case, the focus is not on the creation of knowledge itself but on its active application. In his report "Encouraging a British Invention Revolution", Andrew Witty (2013) claims that universities are responsible for supporting the economic growth and that all institutions have to be encouraged to pursue this goal.

REF 2021 incorporates three main elements:

- **Outputs** – they represent 60 % of the assessment (reduced from 65 % in 2014), and results achieved by a given university during the assessment period (from 1st January 2014 until 31st December 2020) are examined.
- **Impact** – it adds up to 25 % of the assessment (an increase from 20 % in 2014) and encompasses study cases which describe the benefits of university research in detail. Impact is associated with the particular institution where the study has taken place, and it is not considered an achievement of an individual member of the research team.
- **Environment** – which amounts to 15 % of the assessment and describes the framework conditions which have to encourage the performance of research. These include a research strategy, staff development, cooperation both in the academia and outside, equality, and cultural diversity. It also looks at the revenue from the studies conducted and the successfully completed PhD studies.

Universities receive marks for each of those elements and, based on that, a grade point average (GPA) is formed. These elements are assessed for each structural unit at the university (units of assessment) and for the university as a whole. The GPA is the basis for calculating the amount of funding which the university receives.

3. National research assessment practices in EU Member States

This section contains a review of the specific national research assessment practices of several European countries, mainly from Central and Eastern

Europe, representatives of old and new EU members, and different in terms of the implementation of this activity. By the very nature of the type of assessments and the availability of information our analysis is more quantitative than qualitative, but we will be able to draw different conclusions than usually.

3.1. Austria

Regulatory framework

In 2011, the federal government of Austria adopted a strategy for the development of research, technology, and innovations (RTI). The strategy reflects the commitment of the Austrian government to support the development of scientific research, technologies, and innovations. It provides a framework for the goals and measures, the financial commitment for their realisation and the incentives related to it. Work is currently under way on a version of the strategy with a time horizon by 2030. The document focuses on sustainable economic development accompanied by transformations imposed by the new framework conditions. The strategy prioritises support for fundamental research, a reform of the funding model for universities, and increasing the funds attracted from external sources (Ecker et al., 2019).

The latest OECD documents highlight the structural weakness of the Austrian assessment system, which is the result of its limited implementation, including an insufficient access to, and an insufficient interconnectedness of, statistical data in public institutions which have been accumulated based on the financed research. The existing assessment practice does not include enough specific and primary micro data, nor is there a possibility for comparison of the individual sources of information. This leads to methodological limitations which significantly hinder the impact assessment and political interventions in the research field (Ecker et al., 2019). In order to resolve this problem, a Platform for Registry Data Research is being created for the purpose of providing data which correlate to research.

The Austrian Platform for Research and Technology Policy Evaluation functions in parallel, which ensures the transparency needed.

Funding

There are three main institutions which provide funding for scientific research, technologies, and innovations in Austria both on a federal and regional level. The main part of the funding on a federal level is provided by the following institutions: Austrian Science Fund (FWF), The Austrian Research Promotion Agency (FFG), and the Austrian Economic Service (Austria Wirtschaftsservice, AWS).

Public universities in Austria receive funding on the basis of results from negotiations with the Federal Ministry of Education, Research, and Science. A contract is signed for the performance of the commitments within a specific time period. Up until 2019, the federal ministry provided funding to state universities in the form of a fixed budget amount. The universities are free to use these funds providing that they fulfil the commitments agreed with the federal ministry in the respective implementation agreements. The post-2019 reform introduced a new funding system based on the capacity related to student training. The 2019–2020 implementation agreements are the first ones under the new funding system (OECD/European Union, 2019).

The funds provided are allocated in three fields: teaching; scientific research (for science-oriented universities) or progress and arts evaluation (for arts-oriented universities); infrastructural and strategic development. The reference value for the main indicators of the first and second pillar are negotiated in agreements with the higher education institutions. The reference values determine the portion of the joint budget for each university, which is based on specific indicators (OECD/European Union, 2019).

For the purpose of optimising the management of financial instruments, the principal funding structures (FFG and FWF) perform periodic evaluations (Eisenhut, 2020). Different quantitative and qualitative methods are used depending on the objectives and the scope of the evaluation.

Evaluation is the main instrument for an institution such as the FWF, which is required to justify its decisions to many different people: first, to the scientific community ... and finally to the public: the taxpayer has the right to learn what is done with the money that ultimately comes from his or her pocket, and he or she should also expect to have this information communicated in an understandable way. Since its establishment, the FWF has set benchmarks for Austria in regard to the evaluation and decision-making procedures it employs.
Austrian Science Fund (Fonds zur Förderung der wissenschaftlichen Forschung, FWF)

Criteria

Austria uses the OECD/DAC criteria system and standards. The latter encompasses several main criteria – relevance, effectiveness, efficiency, impact, and sustainability.

Specific criteria are also taken into account in the assessment of research in the field of Humanities. They combine a total of 41 measures allocated in 5 theme-based fields: (1) Freedom of research, (2) Quality and measurement of productivity and efficiency, (3) Potential for international outreach, (4) Alternative environment for establishing contacts, and (5) Encouragement of researchers in the early stages of their career.

The following criteria are used in specific cases:

- Coherency: it reflects the coherency of policies and operational coherency (coordination with other participants during the implementation).
- Connectivity: the degree to which short-term humanitarian measures are implemented in a context where long-term and interconnected issues are reported (substituting the sustainability criteria).
- Scope: the extent to which the main vulnerable groups facing life-threatening events are influenced by humanitarian measures.
- Coordination: the extent to which the interventions of different participants are harmonised for the purpose of using synergies and minimising gaps, duplication, and resource-related conflicts (this is often part of the efficiency criteria).

It is important to highlight that in the Austrian research assessment practice there is no need to mechanically apply all possible criteria. Instead, the relevant indicators have to be selected for each individual case in correspondence with the specific expectations, objective, and subject of the assessment.

The research examining different indicators, which are applicable in the performance of research assessment, is accompanied by a short content analysis in regards to the most common terms related to research assessment in the existing national legal data bases.

Content analysis

Source: Authors' own elaboration.

Austria places a clear focus on technologies, and it can be assumed that the research assessment system has a positive effect on the country's economy. Proof of this are commonly used terms such as 'implementation; efficiency; development; economy-related services, sustainability'. The high share of resources provided by the business also contributes to the positive impact on the innovation ecosystem. Naturally, the political significance of these documents is clearly visible through commonly used terms such as research quality, objectives, financial instruments, and curating bodies.

3.2. The Netherlands

Regulatory framework

The research assessment at universities in the Netherlands is regulated by the Higher Education and Research Act, and it is jointly performed on a six-year basis by three institutions: the Association of Universities in the Netherlands (VSNU), the Dutch Research Council (NWO), and the Royal Netherlands Academy of Arts and Sciences (KNAW). They prepare a Strategy Evaluation Protocol (SEP), which must be followed during each upcoming period.

An executive board, which consists of representatives of each university and the authorised organisations NWO and KNAW, decides which year the respective research unit is going to be assessed – institutions, departments, research groups, clusters, etc. The research unit is assessed in relation to the declared targets and the strategy, if there is one. The assessment supports organisations to improve the quality of their research and there is a focus on its benefit for the public.

Funding

Public universities and colleges receive block funding based on the number of research position awarded, including doctoral ones. They are free to decide how to use these funds in order to meet the costs for their ordinary activities: staff, equipment, and student accommodation. In addition, the government provides universities and colleges with subsidies for scientific research.

The grants from the government are not the only source of funding for universities and colleges. They receive financial support on a project-competition basis from the Dutch Research Council (NWO), local and international institutions, and not-for-profit organisations.

Criteria

The main document which forms the basic assessment represents a self-evaluation methodology prepared by the respective research unit. In addition, an assessment based on an on-site visit of the assessment team is prepared. There are three main criteria for the assessment of the research unit: (1) quality of the scientific research, (2) societal relevance, (3) viability.

As regards the quality of the research, it is monitored on an international, national, and, if appropriate, regional level. Research significance, academic prestige, and leadership in the relevant field are accounted for. The assessment is defended through a narrative reasoning by providing suitable evidence. The assessment protocol follows the guidelines of the Declaration on Research Assessment, adopted by the evaluating institutions.

The research assessment also reflects the societal relevance of the research and the commitments undertaken in economic, social, cultural, and any other relevant aspect. A lot more time is needed for the purpose of assessing the social impact; therefore in some cases the assessment can only reflect achievements from a previous period. Where possible, the connection between teaching and scientific research is examined. The key scientific findings and achievements and the subsequent changes are described in a narrative form.

The viability criterion evaluates to what extent the targets of the research unit are scientifically and socially relevant, and it places a focus on whether the plans and resources are adequate in relation to the strategy applied.

Additional or specific criteria are the following: (1) open science, (2) doctoral training policy, (3) academic culture, and (4) human resources policy in accordance with the Strategy Evaluation Protocol 2021–2027. These provide clarity as to how scientific research is performed and how the research unit is managed. The specific criteria are not examined individually but adapted to the main ones. In addition, the evaluating team has the right to decide to what extent each indicator is suitable for the specific case.

The following criteria are also assessed:

- Adherence to the 'Open Science' principles. It is assessed to what extent different stakeholders are included in the preparation and implementation of the strategy of a given research unit and to what extent the researchers are actively communicating with colleagues and public representatives. Subject to assessment are the storing of research data, the accumulation method, and the availability of materials and publications with an open access. Even if the research unit is not following the open science principles, the panel evaluates the plans for their future implementation.
- Subject to evaluation is the research unit's policy on the training of PhD students, the teaching methods, and the existence of a functioning quality and control system for this activity. The content and the structure of doctoral programmes, the candidate selection methods, the enrolment and tutoring, including how students are guided towards the labour market, the number of successful PhD candidates, and their career prospects and success are presented.
- Academic culture – the social security and the inclusion of the academic staff, research integrity, and the methods for creating such an environment are assessed.
- Human resources policy in accordance with the main assessment criteria – it accounts for the presence of cultural diversity in respect to gender, age, ethnic, and cultural origin, for the field of work, and for future action plans in relation to this topic. Units provide information about their

3. National research assessment practices in EU Member States

selection, training, career development, awards, and incentives policy (SEP 2021–2027).

The Royal Netherlands Academy of Arts and Sciences (KNAW) believes that the quality of research cannot be assessed solely on the basis of research publications and citation impact, because this approach is very unsatisfactory for a lot of research fields and the standard assessment methods do not reflect important aspects of research fields such as designs, software in construction disciplines, or books and articles in Dutch which are not included in the citation statistics.

In the wake of the proliferation of quantitative research assessment, prominent initiatives call for an increased focus on practices of responsible research evaluation. These focus on producing research metrics or indicators that adhere to certain principles such as transparency and diversity.
Petersohn et al. (2020)

Content analysis

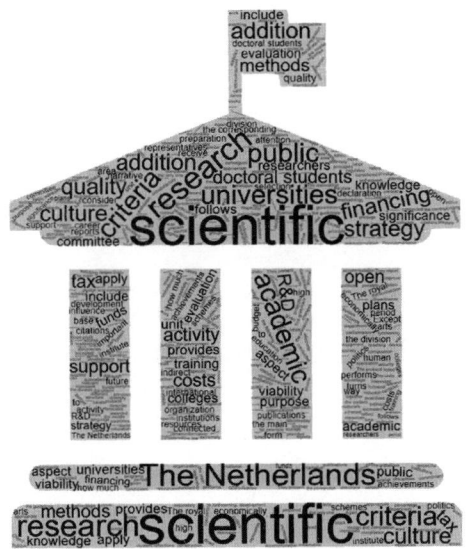

Source: Authors' own elaboration.

The Dutch documents address socio-economic needs (culture, public, open, support) and place a focus on the high quality of research (quality), the research itself, financial instruments and incentives systems, and a clear link with the educational process, including doctoral training.

3.3. Czech Republic

Regulatory framework

The research system in the country is regulated through the 2019–2030 National Innovation Strategy and the Act on the Support of Research and Development of Public Funds (ACT No. 130/2002 Coll. on the Support of Research and Development from Public Funds). Through the 2019–2030 National Innovation Strategy of the Czech Republic the government approves the national priorities of scientific research, experimental development, and innovations. The law in support of R&D defines the forms of research funding, the state authorities responsible for the financing, and the procedures for the allocation and use of the funds. In addition, there are a number of by-laws.

The assessment of the activities conducted by state universities in the field of science and research is performed on the basis of the methodology of the Research, Development, and Innovation Council Department in the Czech Republic (last update in 2017). According to some researchers (Hasprová et al., 2018), the assessment process is complicated and often unpredictable. The conditions for assessing research results often change retroactively, the application of this methodology is limited only to the territory of the country, and it is difficult to ensure benchmarking. According to the authors, the main disadvantage of this assessment practice is its instability or the retroactive change of rules, but also the fact that the assessors can apply a subjective approach. Since the assessment also includes publishing activity, the number of publications increases, but their quality is questionable.

The Methodology for Evaluating Research Organisations and Research, Development, and Innovation Purpose-tied Aid Programmes started being applied after 2017. It aims to:

- accumulate information about the quality management of R&D at all levels and the subsidies foreseen in the longer term, which support a conceptual development of research organisations;
- establish a level of efficiency in the spending of public funds;

- support an increase in the quality and the international competitiveness of R&D;
- guarantee the accountability of stakeholders in R&D.

Funding

The Czech Republic actively encourages scientific research, developments, and innovations through various financial instruments. They are administered by different national institutions (Ministry of Education, Youth and Sport, Ministry of Industry and Trade, the Czech Science Foundation, and the Czech Technology Agency) or targeted EU financial instruments. Various incentives related to the development of R&D are applied in specific cases.

The Czech Science Foundation (also known as the Guarantee Agency of the Czech Republic, GA CR) supports research with a strong potential for achieving results with a high research quality, international research cooperation in the field of fundamental research, professional development of researchers from an early stage, and the efficient use of funding.

A number of incentives are offered in the country. For example, technological centres can receive investment incentives if they meet certain conditions.

Criteria

Research assessment is performed every 5 years and analyses the different missions of research organisations, their results, their impact, and their prospects. The specifics of various fields are accounted for and the institutions are assessed in a national and international context through independent expert assessments. Subject of analysis is also the way in which public funds, which are reserved for institutional development, are allocated. The research assessment is based on several main principles, which include a differentiation on three levels of management, the classification of institutions in three segments (universities, institutes of the Czech Academy of Sciences, research units of organisations), and an assessment of the quality, which suggests a bibliometrics analysis and on-site visits by the institutions.

IV. Comparing research assessment models on a national level

> *Professional and expert panels composed of both Czech and foreign experts have been established for peer-review evaluations and to assess the quality of results ... This approach was recommended by the international audit of research, development, and innovation in the Czech Republic carried out by Technopolis Group in 2011.*
> Good (2015)

The criteria applied are as follows:

Social importance:

- social importance / social benefit, which has been achieved through the work of the unit subject to evaluation (usually preceded by a self-evaluation);
- applied research projects (the unit subject to evaluation presents up to five of its most significant applied research projects conducted during the reporting period, and they present the results achieved or the potential of the project for practical implementation);
- results from other applied research;
- cooperation beyond the academic environment, including with business structures and transfer of technologies;
- recognition among the research community;
- actions aimed at promoting the research of the unit subject of evaluation.

Viability – this criterion assesses the research environment and the quality of management and internal processes of the university or the unit, as follows:

- organisation, control and support for research activity;
- availability of PhD programmes;
- national and international cooperation and mobility;
- human resources and career;
- structure of financial flows which support research, availability of a strategy for attracting funds through implementation of projects of a different scale;
- start-up development strategy;
- availability of research infrastructure and its quality;
- good practices applied in research.

Strategy and policy – this criterion assesses:

- the mission and vision for research development;
- the strategy and objectives for research development;

- instruments for the implementation of the research strategy;
- research examined in a national and international context.

Content analysis

Source: Authors' own elaboration.

The analysis of the documentary data base in the Czech Republic shows that there is a significance attached to the innovation system, the methodological approach, financing, and research and development, but there is a clear interest in international scientific research. The funding of technological activities is also one of the political interests of the state. Some of the priority terms, incorporated in its documents, are also quality, institutional structure, and organisations which curate research.

3.4. Hungary

Regulatory framework

The main document which regulates research development is the Research and Innovation Development Strategy. Its main objectives are as follows: to encourage research groups which conduct research according to international quality standards, to accelerate international research integration, to support knowledge-intensive SMEs, etc.

The authority responsible for the development and implementation of the research policy is the National Research, Development, and Innovation Office (NRDIO). It is an independent organisation which is not under the control of a particular ministry, which differentiates it from the practice in other European countries.

In 2016, the European Commission published an expert assessment of the R&D and innovations system in Hungary. It states that in order to improve the achievements and the competitiveness of the Hungarian research system a focus should be placed on project and competition-related funding due to the existing structural weaknesses in the funding of the research system until now (European Union, 2016). This required the establishment of a new administrative structure to coordinate policies promoting research and innovations development.

Funding

State funding of scientific research in Hungary is provided by the National Research, Development, and Innovations Fund (NRDI Fund).

The main sources of funding for the Hungarian research system are:

- the National Research, Development, and Innovations Office (NKFIA), which consists of two funds: Research and Technological Innovation Fund (KTIA) and Hungarian Scientific Research Fund (OTKA);
- structural funds through their operational programmes and targeted schemes.

In Hungary, more than half of the funds for research and development are provided by the private sector (reaching 53 % in for 2018); the funds from the public sector represent approximately one third of the total amount of expenses. Private companies are the main innovators, over 70 % of the funds for research and development are absorbed by them. Higher education institutions and research institutions receive 13 % of the funds for R&D (Moldicz, 2020).

In 2020, NRDI was divided into two parts. The Research unit finances community-oriented research projects and programmes in support of high achievements in higher education and research institutions and of individual researchers. The Innovations unit supports business innovations and market-oriented research; the cooperation between the business and academics is supported through different investment programmes.

The National Research, Development, and Innovations Fund assess the project proposals which are announced based on a multi-phase evaluation system in accordance with its regulatory framework.

Criteria

The assessment criteria for the results of individual researchers are defined pursuant to decree No. 395/2015. Based on the decree, the employees at higher education institutions undergo a regular efficiency evaluation. The applicable evaluation criteria analyse:

- educational and research results;
- other activities related to educational activity, such as supervision of dissertations;
- publication and patenting of results from research;
- promotion of science and participation in conferences with a guarantee for publishing the articles approved for the report;
- visibility on international data bases;
- funds attracted for the purpose of conducting research;
- active contribution towards the development of young and gifted scholars and doctoral studies;
- results from students' evaluation of the study process;
- public activities.

Researchers from higher education institutions are not evaluated based on their public impact, the commercialisation of results from research, and entrepreneurial activities. No incentives for engaging in industrial participation or the transfer of technologies are offered.

Researchers working at the institutes of the Hungarian Academy of Sciences are evaluated based on procedures and criteria determined by internal regulations, whereas the common standards for university employees do not apply to them.

... most importantly, the experts tasked with evaluating individual researchers' performance should look behind the curtain and examine the qualitative aspects of researchers' publications.
Csomós (2021)

IV. Comparing research assessment models on a national level

Content analysis

The review of the documentary data base in Hungary has found that importance is attached to activities related to innovations, standards, funding and financial instruments, and science and research, but also to efficiency and implementation method. This also corresponds to the new vision of the country aimed at improving the innovation ecosystem.

Source: Authors' own elaboration.

3.5. Bulgaria

Regulatory framework
Due to the diverse national innovation system which covers universities, two national horizontal research structures, both of which function under a specific law – the Bulgarian Academy of Sciences (BAS) and the National Centre for Agrarian Science (NCAS) – research institutes which are part of different ministries, and research-based companies, there are a number of legislative acts adopted in the country: Promotion of Research Act, Higher Education Act, 2017–2030 National Research Development Strategy of the Republic of Bulgaria, Bulgarian Academy of Sciences Act, the Law and structural framework of the National Centre for Agrarian Science, and the Ordinance on the conditions and procedure for assessment, planning,

allocation and spending of the funds of the state budget for the purpose of financing the ordinary research or artistic activity of state higher education institutions. Each year, an assessment of the results from the research or artistic activities of higher education institutions is performed, and based on this assessment the funds for research in state higher education institutions are allocated.

There are also rules for the assessment of scientific research, applicable to higher education institutions and two horizontal research organisations (BAS and NCAS), but there are still no sustainable and systemic results from the assessment for a longer monitoring period because the initiative is part of a pilot project and is only implemented for one year.

The European Commission supported the country through a new assessment instrument, PSF, in the years 2015–2018. This mechanism allowed for the performance of a summative analysis of the state of the national research system, and important recommendations and proposals were made for improving the research ecosystem (Vutsova et al., 2021).

It is good that the strategy mentions the need to involve foreign researchers in an objective accreditation ... a European assessment is required – one which is performed by universities which are more advanced than the Bulgarian ones.
Dichev (2020)

Funding

The funds for research promotion are provided by the state budget and by other sources in line with the targets and priorities established in the National Research Strategy. The state provides the funds for the implementation of national research programmes and projects and supports the creation of a research infrastructure and the access to electronic research data bases.

The National Research Fund is the second financial source for supporting scientific research. Additional sources of funding are operational programmes under the Structural Funds, European Programmes as framework programmes (Horizon 2020, Horizon Europe, COST), other initiatives which support scientific research and innovations (INTERREG, Central and East European Initiative, etc.), programmes promoting bi-lateral research cooperation, etc.

IV. Comparing research assessment models on a national level

Criteria

The assessment criteria systems of the individual research organisations are similar but not entirely identical. An independent external assessment – although not comprehensive – of universities is carried out by the National Evaluation and Accreditation Agency and also through the university ranking system, which includes a research assessment component. BAS and NCAS are assessed internally and independently, while the other research institutes do not have a structured assessment system. In this sense, Bulgaria does not have a uniform research assessment system.

The criteria which are most frequently applied to different research structures cover the following assessment groups:

- Bibliographical (publications, including monographs, share of publications in co-authorship with institutions in other countries, independent citations visible in international data bases).
- Patents and useful models (registered patent applications and a list of registered patents extracted from international data bases according to the up-to-date list of the organisations which are subject to evaluation).
- Funds attracted (under national and international programmes/projects, contracts with Bulgarian or foreign enterprises and/or organisations, license agreements with companies/agricultural producers for the purpose of creating intellectual products).
- Results with regards to the academic development in Bulgaria (successful defence of dissertations, including the acquisition of an academic title as 'doctor of sciences', availability of an up-to-date strategy for the research development of the organisations).

Part of the recommendations under the Policy Support Facility (PSF)
• We recommend the adoption of a broader view on the term 'quality' with regards to research, and also, by taking into account the importance of research for the industry and society, to perceive it as inherent to the concept of 'quality' of the research and in the case of 'targeted' fundamental research.
• We recommend making the necessary corrections in the assessment methodology before using it for the allocation of institutional funding for research. Significant improvements are needed, especially in the approach towards the normalisation of data according to research fields, the definition of indicators and the definition and the differentiation of data sources.
• The current use and design of the scientific impact' indicators should undergo a thorough review. It is our opinion that the use of indicators based on the journal impact factor (JIF), and the h-index, is ill-advised. We recommend that these indicators be excluded from the assessment methodology.
• We recommend to the Bulgarian authorities to review the practice abroad and to apply foreign professional practice on a wider scale. We especially recommend to look for the support of experts on bibliometrics for the purpose of designing citation indicators.
• We recommend developing an assessment system which will ensure uniform impact of indicators in the calculation of evaluations according to assessment criteria, as well as an improvement of the strategic value of the results from the assessment and transparency of the assessment process.
Peer Review of the Bulgarian Research and Innovation system, 2015 under the Horizon 2020 Policy Support Facility

Since the beginning of 2022, the Ministry of Education and Science initiated a redesign of assessment criteria towards research quality. The main impetus is given upon the quantitative criteria, and severe debate was started this year.

Content analysis

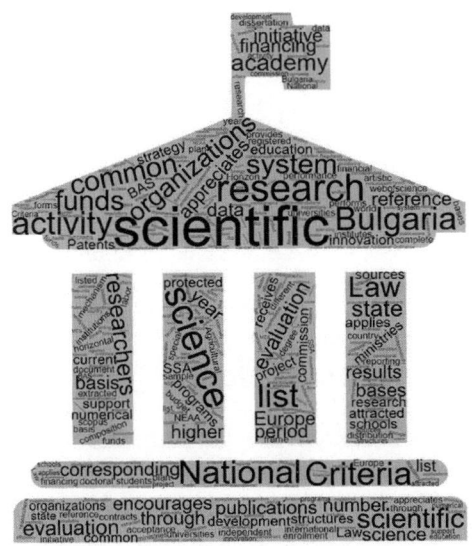

Source: Authors' own elaboration.

In the national strategic documents, Bulgaria places a clear focus on national criteria, which is related to national policy, publications, and science and research; the importance of organisations curating research is also evident. Interestingly enough, concepts such as 'innovation system' and 'technologies' are almost absent.

3.6. Poland

Regulatory framework

The main regulatory framework in Poland includes the Higher Education and Science Act, also known as the Science Constitution, or Act 2.0, adopted in October 2018. The Act imposes significant changes in the research system: it creates better conditions for research and didactic achievements, ensures the sustainable development of the academic centres in the whole country, introduces doctoral schools, and provides universities with the suitable tools necessary for an efficient management. Research is in line with the national strategy, the Strategy for Innovative and Efficient Economy – Dynamic Poland 2020, in force for the 2013–2020 period, and with the Programme for the Development of Higher Education and Science for the years 2015–2030. The following four main measures are foreseen according to this last programme:

- increase in the quality of training at higher education institutions, which should be adapted to social and economic needs;
- improvement of the quality of the research conducted at national research institutions;
- reforms in the organisation, management, and funding of higher education and science;
- a more tangible impact of research on the social and economic environment.

The data about the results from the activities of Polish researchers and higher education institutions are collected through an integrated system (Information System on Higher Education – POL-on) (Euraxess Poland), created in 2011 in order to guarantee real accountability and transparency with regards to the efficiency of public spending for science and education.

The main participants in the national innovation system are universities and research institutes, but also commercial and not-for-profit companies of different sizes. There are over 400 public and private universities in

Poland, and the national research system also includes the following institutions: National Agency for Academic Exchange, National Centre for Research and Development, and National Science Centre (Ministry of Science and Higher Education, Poland).

Funding

Research funding is mainly provided through the state budget in the form of statutory funding and grants. They are primarily granted to institutions of the Ministry of Education and Science depending on the results from the national assessment which is performed every 4 years. The level of funding depends on the category awarded to the institution.

Block subsidies for university departments amount to around 10 % of their annual budget, while for fundamental and applied research institutes it is up to 30 % of their annual budget.

The National Centre for Research and Development finances the implementation of national and international programmes, including strategic programmes, which implement the state research and innovation policy. The centre allocates funds under operational programmes for the 2014–2020 financial framework: Operational Programme 'Smart Growth' (SG OP), Operational Programme 'Knowledge Education Development' (KED OP), and a beneficiary under Operational Programme 'Digital Poland' (PO PC).

The Polish National Agency for Academic Exchange (NAWA) funds activities related to the process of internationalisation in Polish higher education institutions and research institutions, and it supports the establishment of international partnerships, capacity-building, and the creation of the relevant organisational infrastructure.

The National Research Centre supports fundamental research; it funds research projects implemented by researchers and/or research teams and post-doctoral internships and provides PhD scholarships.

Additional funds are attracted from European structural funds and framework programmes for research and development: Horizon 2020, Horizon Europe, and other European initiatives.

Criteria

Research assessment focuses on four basic criteria: research and artistic achievements (for example, monographs, journal articles, patents), research potential, material effects from the research (for example, external financing) and other effects/results from research, and a few specific elements ('accents') presented by the unit which is subject to evaluation (Kulczycki et al., 2020). Publications (national and international) account for 60 to 80 % of the total research efficiency of the unit which is subject to evaluation. The number of citations, however, especially international ones, do not have a significant impact. Apart from publications, data about several other parameters are collected for assessment purposes (Korytkowski & Kulczycki, 2019).

The assessment criteria also include:

- a selected number of publications presented by the research unit and their authors;
- a limited number of research books;
- editorial participation in research editorial teams;
- articles in science journals, indexed in JCR or ERIH;
- recognised patents (patent applications are not taken into account in the assessment).

Content analysis

Based on the documents in Poland, apart from the main terms related to research, the following stand out: research quality on a European level, scope, targeting, institutional structure, funding, including private, and the tools for that; also a correlation between the educational process and the regulatory framework was established. There is no clear focus on innovations or technologies, but there is one on the development and the role of business as represented by company structures of a different calibre.

Source: Authors' own elaboration.

3.7. Lithuania

Regulatory framework

The main law in Lithuania which regulates research is the Law on Higher Education and Research (2009, updated as of 2017). There is also the Research and Innovation Smart Specialisation Strategy, and the Guidelines for the evaluation of research and experimental development and artistic activities of Lithuania, approved by the Ministry of Education, Science, and Sport, are also covered by the regulatory framework. The institution which prepares recommendations on the development of national research and higher education, monitors and analyses their condition, and participates the implementation of various policies is the Research and Higher Education Monitoring and Analysis Centre (MOSTA). In addition, there are a number of by-laws regulating the functioning of the research system in the country.

Lithuania applies a dual research assessment system:

- annual, which is based on statistics of the results from research in terms of publications, patents, and other applications, and

- an international reference assessment, which is qualitative and is entirely performed by international experts every five years.

Funding

The Ministry of Education, Science, and Sport funds higher education institutions and research institutions on the basis of the results from the assessment, which is performed every 5 years. 60 % of the funds for research are allocated according to the quality parameters of a comparative expert assessment, and the remaining 40 %, according to the quantity indicators of the official assessment. Funding according to this assessment model has been provided to research and educational institutions since 2019.

Criteria

The criteria system in Lithuania consists of three types of criteria:

- quality of the scientific research – which is assessed in a given research field or group of research fields;
- economic and social impact – which is assessed only in the field of the research;
- potential for development.

Data which have to be provided depending on the research field include:

1. List of the best results from the research;
2. List of the best reports presented at conferences abroad;
3. List of the most important national and international awards for research and development received;
4. Data about PhD students;
5. List with the results from research which have had the biggest social and economic impact, and the requests for R&D by the business sector (both Lithuanian and foreign);
6. List of the most important participations of researchers representing the unit which is subject to assessment, in working groups or panels created by state authorities, state or municipal institutions and organisations, and companies;
7. List of the consultations provided by the unit which is subject to assessment to the public or economic actors;
8. List of the most important research conferences and events organised by the unit, which is subject to assessment;

9. List of the most important memberships in editorial teams of science journals by researchers representing the unit which is subject to assessment;
10. List of the most important memberships in international working groups and associations, participation in international expert groups, etc. by researchers representing the unit which is subject to assessment;
11. List of the most important results from the promotion of science.

Content analysis

Source: Authors' own elaboration.

The main focus in Lithuania is placed on research development on an international level, its quality, funding, and the institutional environment. Research is examined in the context of economic results. Interestingly enough, the organisations curating this activity are missing from the priority terms.

3.8. Slovenia

Regulatory framework

The main documents relating to the performance of scientific research in Slovenia are the Resolution on the Strategy for Research and Innovation in Slovenia, completed in 2020, an Open Access Strategy and a Road Map for Scientific Research Infrastructure, a 2021–2030 Research Strategy, the Scientific Research and Development Act, a Decision for the establishment of a public research agency of the Republic of Slovenia, a National

Research and Development Programme and the creation of a European Research Area, and a Guidance on (co)funding and assessment procedures for scientific research and monitoring of the implementation of scientific research. The Resolution on the 2021–2030 Scientific Research and Innovations Strategy in Slovenia is due to be adopted.

The Ministry of Education, Science, and Sport, the Slovenian Research Agency (ARRS), and the Research and Technologies Strategic Council are responsible for the development and coordination of the research policy. The Research Agency is an independent organisation for public funding and provides tools which allow for a stable funding of scientific achievements.

Funding

Research funding supports the following types of research:

- research programmes;
- fundamental, applied, and doctoral research projects;
- training of young researchers in research organisations;
- international cooperation in the field of research;
- attracting recognised foreign researchers.

Research and development funding is provided through the state budget and from other sources in line with the objectives and priorities indicated in the Research and Innovations Strategy. Institutions participating in the provision of funds are the Slovenian Research Agency, the Slovenian Public Agency for Entrepreneurship, Innovation, Development, Investment, and Tourism, and the Slovene Science Foundation. In addition to national funds, funding under operational programmes through European Structural Funds is also provided.

Criteria

The assessment criteria system includes:

- funds attracted for the implementation of projects requested by businesses;
- funds attracted from projects financed by the EU and other international organisations;
- funds acquired through national or municipal budgets;
- number of new products, technologies, services, or concepts with an innovation potential and which have been developed or implemented in local or foreign companies;

- number of international patents applications and number of acquired patents;
- funds acquired through the transfer of copyrights on technologies or patents, samples or a specialised one-of-a-kind product/system and technological demonstrations;
- publication of a research monograph by publishers recommended by the agency;
- articles in impact factor journals.

The Slovenian model of research evaluation needs to be understood in light of the specific challenges which small research communities face and of its specific historical background. It is hence relevant that the bibliometric system affords certain advantages in terms of objectivity and transparency in a situation where research funds are limited and where consistent quality review by peers, domestic or international, is difficult.
Hojnik (2019)

Content analysis

A similarity with the terms used by Austria is observed in Slovenian documents. Apart from the compulsory presence of research, funding, and funding instruments, criteria, organisational/institutional environment, the role of technologies, and patent activity, which contribute to the country's economic development, is also evident.

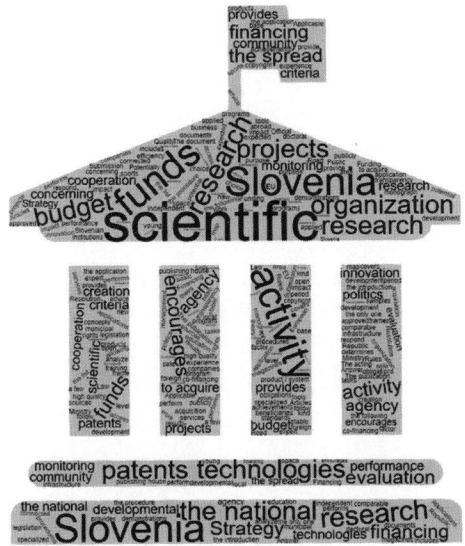

Source: Authors' own elaboration.

IV. Comparing research assessment models on a national level

The countries which are subject to this study are examined and compared based on the main factors which influence the innovation ecosystem: regulatory framework, funding including incentives, and the existence of a system for ensuring accountability to the society, i.e., assessment procedures and main assessment indicators. Table 4.1. presents these key factors. It clearly shows the differences which indirectly characterise the status of each country as an innovator.

Table 4.1: Key factors of the national innovation ecosystems

Country	Regulatory framework			Funding			Assessment		Criteria	
	General	Specific	High level of coordination with the remaining legal basis	Public	Private	Public/private ratio	Compulsory	Optional	Additional	Compulsory
Austria	☑	☑	yes	☑	☑	bigger share of private funding	☑			☑
Bulgaria	☑	☑	no	☑	☑	bigger share of public funding	☑			☑
The Czech Republic	☑	☑	relatively coordinated	☑	☑	comparable	☑			☑
Hungary	☑	☑	yes	☑	☑	bigger share of private funding	☑			☑
Lithuania	☑	☑	relatively coordinated	☑	☑	bigger share of public funding	☑			☑
Netherlands	☑	☑	yes	☑	☑	bigger share of private funding	☑		☑	☑
Poland	☑	☑	yes	☑	☑	comparable	☑			☑
Slovenia	☑	☑	yes	☑	☑	comparable	☑			☑

Source: Authors' own elaboration.

Based on the above, each country works with a different volume of legal documents, general and specific (e.g., special laws), but part of them is not coordinated with the remaining relevant documents due to the fact that community research policy is a horizontal one, and there is no obligation for full synchronisation. In some countries given documents are the result of an accidental initiative. In all of the countries studied, funding consists of both public and private sources; however, the ratio between the public and the private sources varies significantly per country. A significant share of private investments is observed in Austria and the Netherlands. The criteria system applied also varies per country. Additional criteria, apart

4. Main research assessment indicators influencing the innovation ecosystem

from the basic ones, are applied in the Netherlands, while in Austria it is not compulsory to consider all of the indicators of the criteria system.

4. Main research assessment indicators influencing the innovation ecosystem

The next section presents various dissections of comparisons between the research assessment systems of the individual countries, and different aspects are visualised. National practices are compared with a focus on the criteria used. The participation of the countries in the Seventh Framework Programme and Horizon 2020 is discussed, both in terms of the number of projects supported and in terms of the funding share; such data demonstrate the ability of research organisations to attract external funding, which is a clear evidence of their research capacity and competitiveness.

Figure 4.1 illustrates the diversity of indicators which are applied in the research assessment of the individual countries and shows their relative significance.

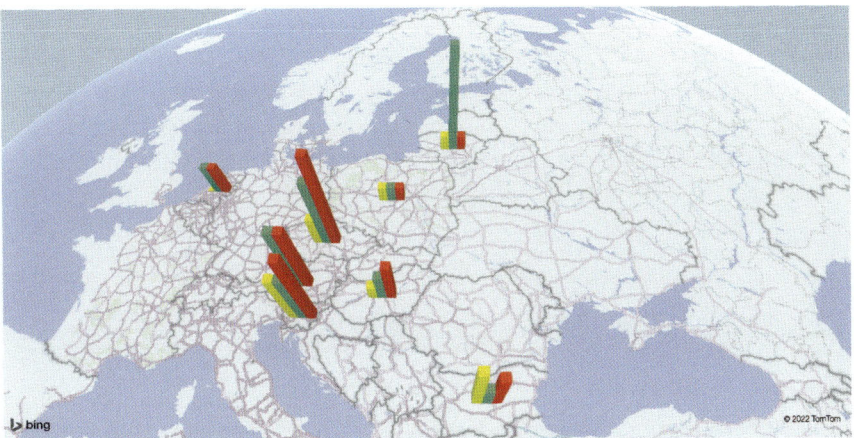

Source: Authors' own elaboration based on national documents.

Figure 4.1: *Number of indicators which are assessed in research assessments*[17]
Source: authors

The significance of human resources is more clearly defined as an indicator with impact in the old Member States (the Netherlands and Austria).

---

17 Yellow: number of bibliometric indicators; green: number of human resources indicators; red: number of infrastructure indicators.

IV. Comparing research assessment models on a national level

In the Czech Republic, Austria, Slovenia, and Hungary the existence of a contemporary research infrastructure also plays an important role. In Poland, there is a relative balance between the three categories of indicators under review, and only in Bulgaria there is a distinct inclination towards bibliometrics. Despite that, the national standards in Bulgaria only imitate what 'in the West' is understood as bibliometrics; thus an article in a top-ranking journal equals three reports at local conferences, which publish all of the proceedings. Bibliographical criteria receive the least attention in the Netherlands and Austria, but they are included in the quality assessment.

The functioning of the assessment system through the prism of the number of indicators, which is relevant to the size of the markers, is illustrated in Figure 4.2. This is a comparison of relatively aggregated indicators allocated in several main groups.

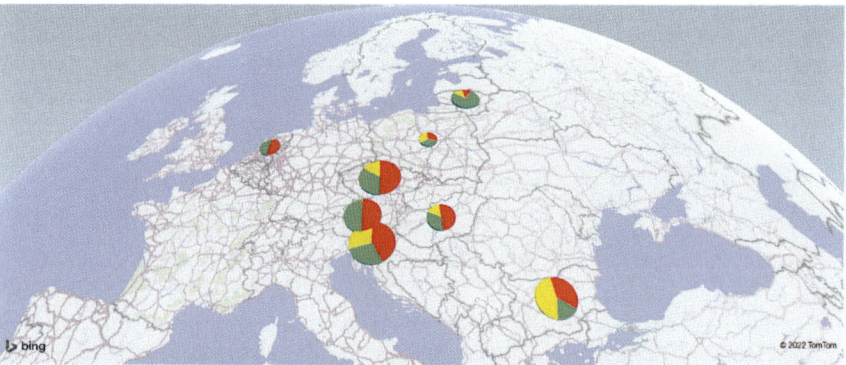

Source: Authors' own elaboration based on data from Innovation Scoreboard.

Figure 4.2: Research assessment (based on groups of indicators)[18]

The new Member States (Bulgaria, Hungary, and Slovenia) apply more indicators compared to the EU-15 countries. This can be explained with the lack of a systemic and holistic assessment practices and a search for the most suitable one; so this characteristic can truly reflect the up-to-date state of the research system.

Figure 4.3 shows the impact of the different categories of indicators; the size of the markers corresponds to the impact of the bibliometric indicators.

---

18 Yellow: number of bibliometric indicators; green: number of human resources indicators; red: number of infrastructure indicators.

4. Main research assessment indicators influencing the innovation ecosystem

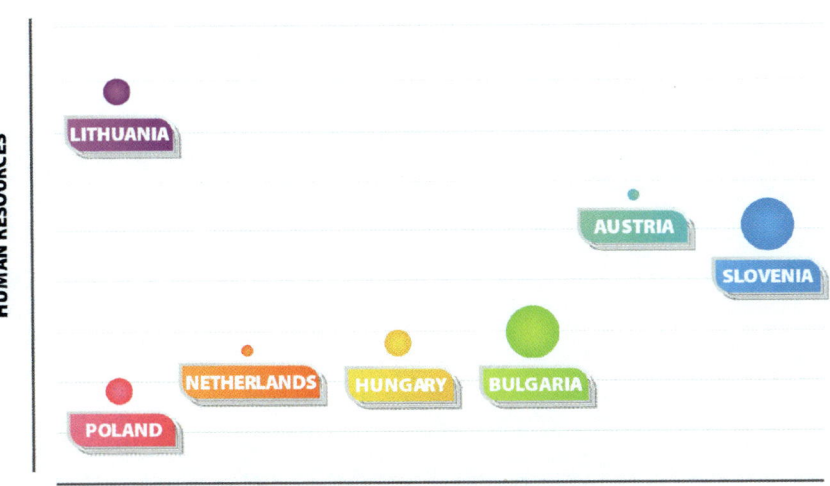

Source: Authors' own elaboration.

Figure 4.3: Distribution of the categories of research indicators according to impact

Slovenia and Bulgaria attribute the highest level of importance to bibliometrics, but Slovenia ranks high the availability of a modern research infrastructure. In Lithuania, the quality of human resources is especially important, while the other countries maintain a relatively good balance with regards to the importance of the individual criteria. Austria and the Netherlands do not consider bibliometrics as especially important indicators.

Figure 4.4 illustrates the significance of the different categories of indicators used in the performance of research assessment in the countries under review. Bulgaria's preference towards bibliometrics is evident, but we need to note once again that these do not necessarily reflect quality. Years ago, Romania managed to increase the quality of Romanian research thanks to well-formulated bibliometrics, incentives, and sanctions related thereto.

IV. Comparing research assessment models on a national level

Source: Authors' own elaboration.

Figure 4.4: Level of importance of different indicators

As is illustrated in Figure 4.5, we observe a declining relationship between the assessments and the results for the criterion bibliometrics.

4. Main research assessment indicators influencing the innovation ecosystem

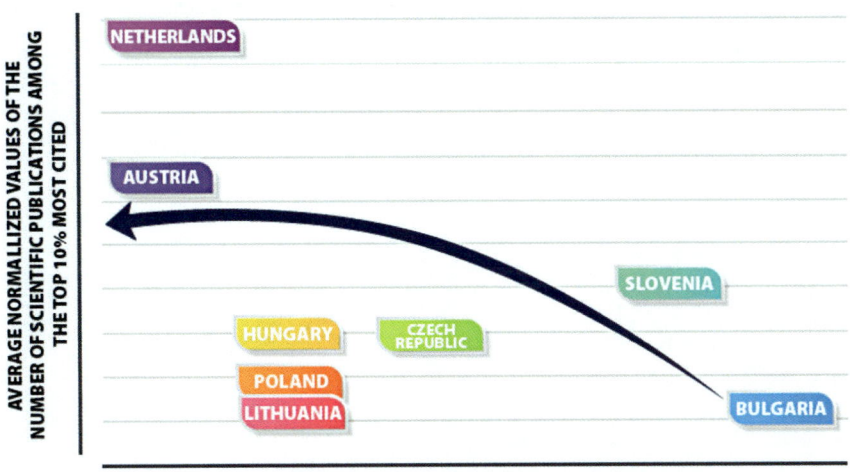

Source: Authors' own elaboration based on data from Innovation Scoreboard.

Figure 4.5: The link between assessment and results for bibliometrics

There was a search for a link between the importance of bibliometric indicators and their impact on researchers' publication activity. Our study analysed the link between the number of the bibliometric indicators applied and the average normalised values of the number of articles in the 10 % of the most cited.

Regardless of the focus which Bulgaria places on bibliometrics, the country has the lowest number of cited articles in comparison to the other countries. The opposite trend is also observed: both Austria and the Netherlands, where the importance of bibliometric indicators is the lowest, are best positioned in terms of publication activity. One plausible explanation of this state of affairs lies in the specific academic culture. In Austria and the Netherlands, the underlying expectation is that a quality paper with new ideas and concepts would be referenced and its authors would be credited. In Bulgaria the culture is a bit different. Even the PhD students might not refer to papers of their advisors[19]. Ideas are often borrowed as one's own, and citations would rather be on empirical data instead of conceptual ideas or purely on personal relationships (you cite a friend even if the source is

---

19   This was prior to the introduction of minimal citation requirements for career development. After that a huge influx is observed.

IV. Comparing research assessment models on a national level

not relevant to the study). This directly undermines the importance of the 'human resources' factor.

Figure 4.6 illustrates the dependency between the impact of the indicators which evaluate human resources and the level of employment in knowledge-intensive sectors.

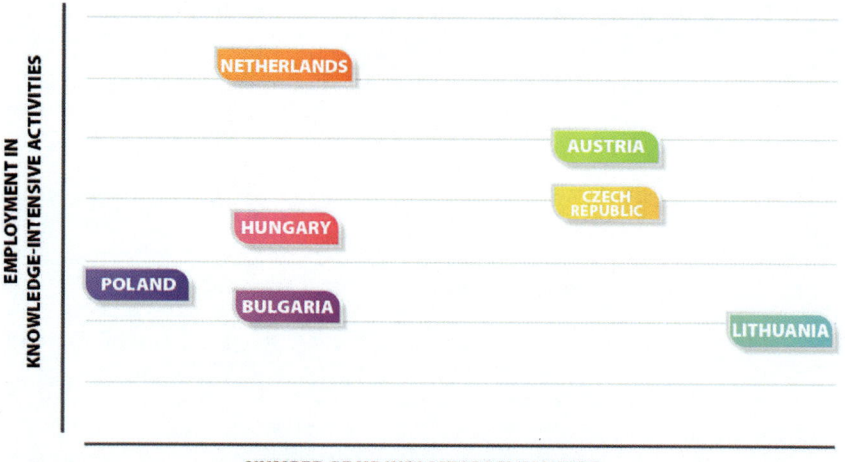

Source: Authors' own elaboration based on data from Innovation Scoreboard.

Figure 4.6: Dependency between the number of HR indicators and the employment in knowledge-intensive industries

There is no clear link which can be applied to all of the countries subject to the analysis. As was observed, there is a clearly defined relation between these indicators in the Netherlands, and we see a certain dependency with regards to the indicators studied in Austria and the Czech Republic, but, at the same time, a discrepancy between both comparable indicators in Lithuania. As for Bulgaria, a clear focus on the importance of human resources is lacking, and, respectively, there is no clear trend with regards to the employment in knowledge-intensive sectors.

4. Main research assessment indicators influencing the innovation ecosystem

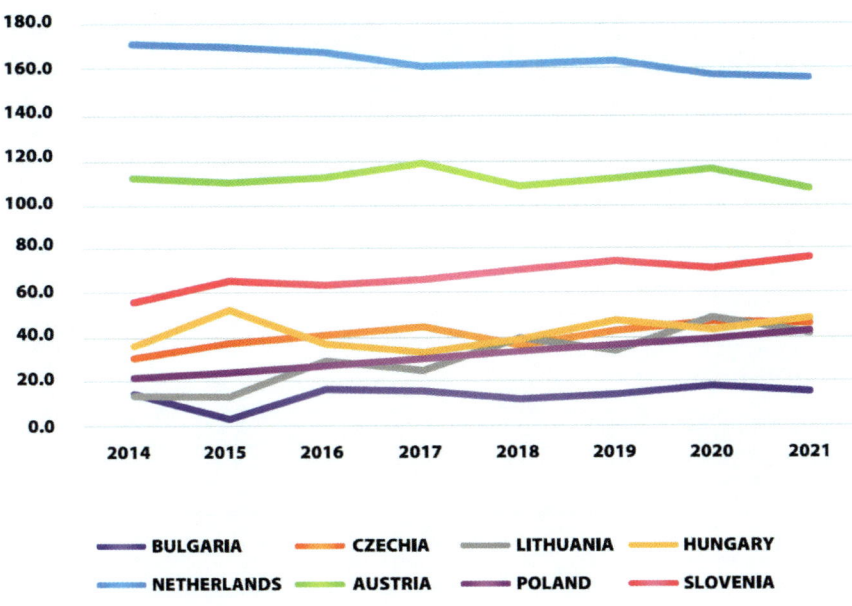

Source: Innovation Scoreboard.

Figure 4.7: Scientific publications among the top 10 % most cited relative to EU in 2014

As concerns the citability of research publication in the top 10 %, Austria and the Netherlands are the leaders. An increase for this indicator is observed in Slovenia, which remains a level above the other countries reviewed here. For most of them there has been a moderate increase over the years. Regardless of the efforts in relation to the research assessment with a focus on bibliography, Bulgaria has the lowest share of articles among the most cited ones. It is evident that the old Member States, which have a more open assessment system, remain at the top and continue keeping this trend.

IV. Comparing research assessment models on a national level

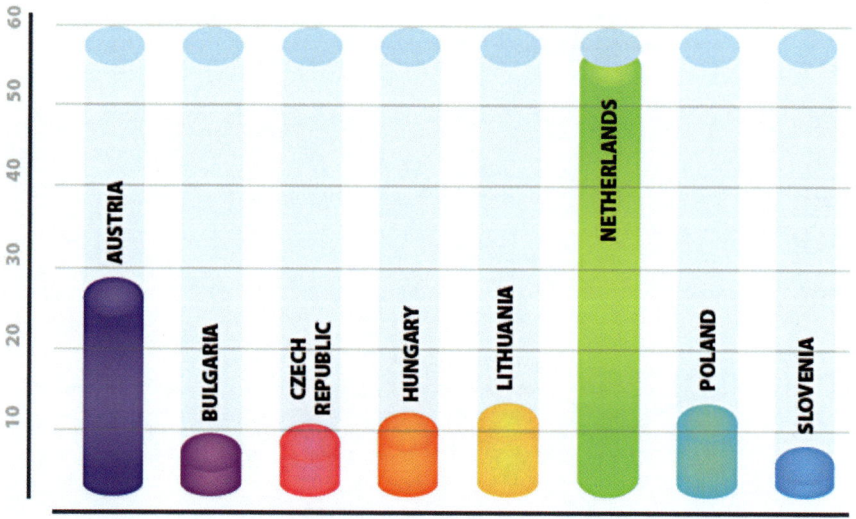

Source: Scimago.

Figure 4.8: H-index per country, 2020

The countries with the highest H-index are again the Netherlands and Austria. The other countries have relatively similar indicators. The data for Bulgaria, which are not the most favourable, show that, despite having a clear focus on the importance of bibliographical data and the introduction of respective incentives, no notable progress is reported.

4. Main research assessment indicators influencing the innovation ecosystem

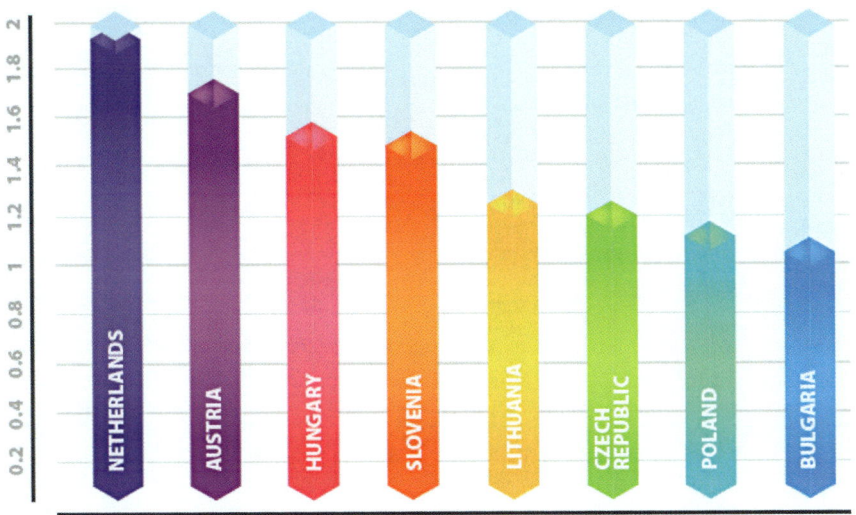

Source: InCites, Web of Science, 2022.

Figure 4.9: Impact Relative to World

'Impact Relative to World' is an indicator published by InCites, Web of Science. It reflects the impact of citations as a ratio to the average impact of this criterion for the world over the last 5 years. According to this specific criterion, the best positioned countries are once again the Netherlands and Austria; Hungary and Slovenia have relatively good indicators, and Bulgaria has the lowest ranking. The latter suggests that the criteria system applied in Bulgaria has to be reconsidered.

IV. Comparing research assessment models on a national level

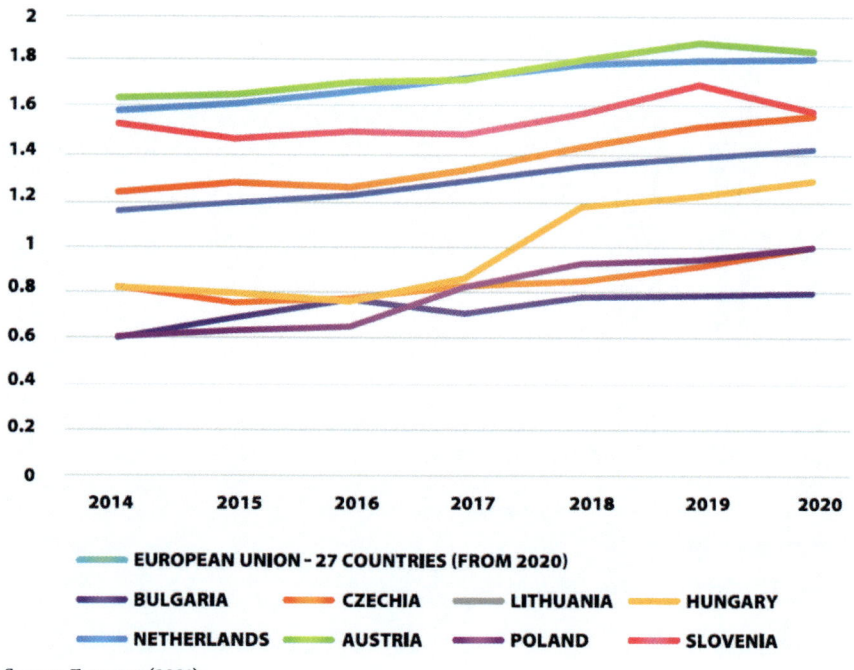

Source: Eurostat (2021).

Figure 4.10: Employees in R&D

Figure 4.10 reflects the trend with regards to the staff employed in R&D as a percentage of the population in the work force equivalent to a full-time job. Austria has the best indicators, followed by the Netherlands, which also has higher indicators with regards to the H-index and Impact Relative to World. A positive trend is observed in Hungary which, to a certain extent, is related to the above-mentioned good indicators. The case of Slovenia is interesting: despite having a lower H-index, it is better positioned with regards to Impact Relative to World, but this is again relevant to the good positions with regards to its research staff.

4. Main research assessment indicators influencing the innovation ecosystem

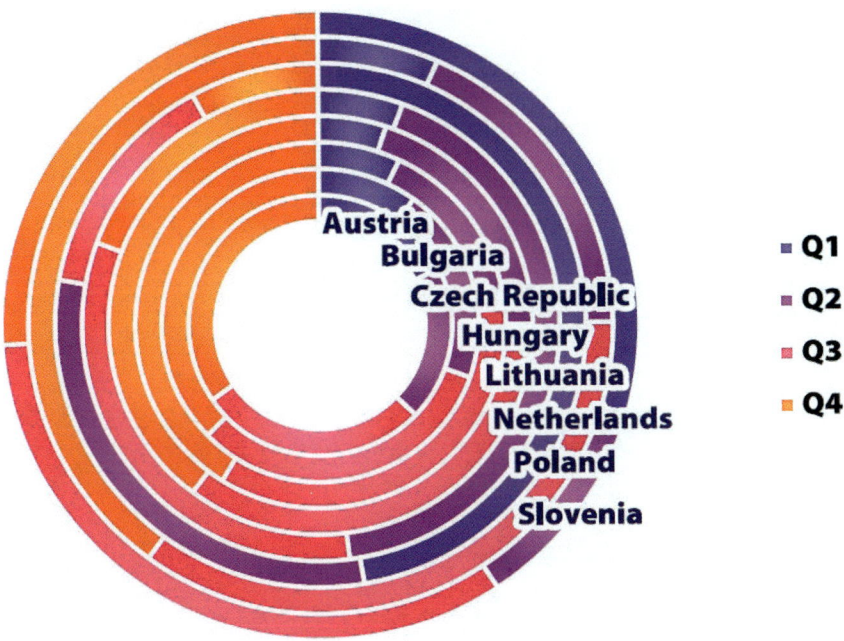

Source: Scimago.

Figure 4.11: Share of publications in the individual quartiles, 2020

Figure 4.11 above illustrates the share of journals for each country in the individual quartiles of Scopus, where quartile 1 contains the most prestigious and cited journals, and quartile 4, the ones with the lowest citation rate. The Netherlands again has the best indicators. Bulgaria occupies a middle position in this ranking. Attention should be brought to the fact that the push for publications in more prestigious international journals further marginalises national journals, many of which are not indexed in international data bases or have a low impact factor; consequently, they are unattractive to domestic authors. It would be a good idea for the responsible authorities involved in policymaking to balance the focus on bibliographical indicators by introducing incentives for the development of quality national science journals.

In specific sectors, though, you might have quite surprising results. Bulgarian social science researchers and those in aesthetics and art criticism,

IV. Comparing research assessment models on a national level

for instance[20], will feel under-represented in the global databases, but the reality is that Bulgaria is ranked 12th by publications in category 'art' (by searching art in Web of Science) in 2021 with results close to Germany and Netherlands. This is since *Art Readings*, a journal, which publishes papers from an annual conference, was included in Emerging Sources of Web of Science.

Figure 4.12 shows that the countries with the highest share of publications in quartile 1, which contains the most prestigious journals in Web of Science, are the Netherlands and Austria, followed by Hungary, Slovenia, and the Czech Republic. The highest percentage of publications in quartile 4 is typical for Bulgaria.

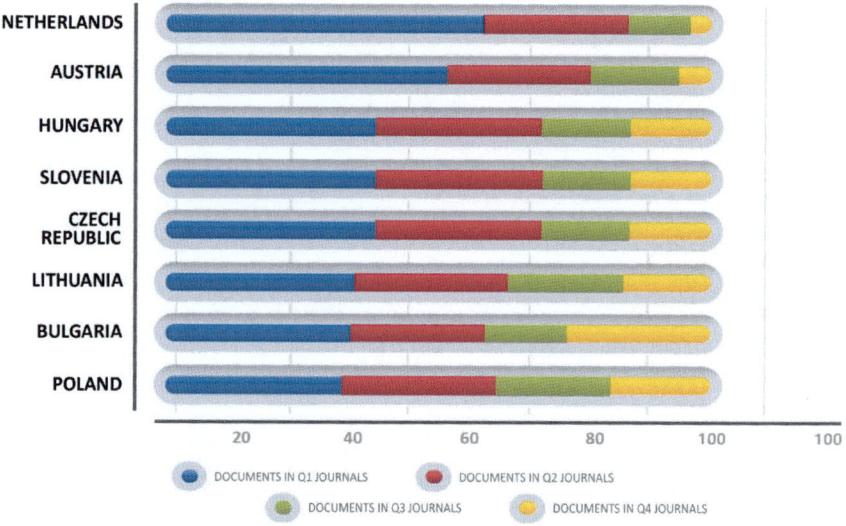

Source: InCites, Web of Science, 2022.

Figure 4.12:   Percentage of documents in journals from the individual quartiles of Web of Science

The following figures examine the countries' capability to attract financial resources from EC framework research and innovation programmes.

---

20 Petar Plamenov (2017) is regarded one of the best national opera and ballet critics, teaching and publishing in aesthetics fields with authoritative articles and books in Bulgaria, but he has never published in outlets visible in Web of Science and Scopus.

4. Main research assessment indicators influencing the innovation ecosystem

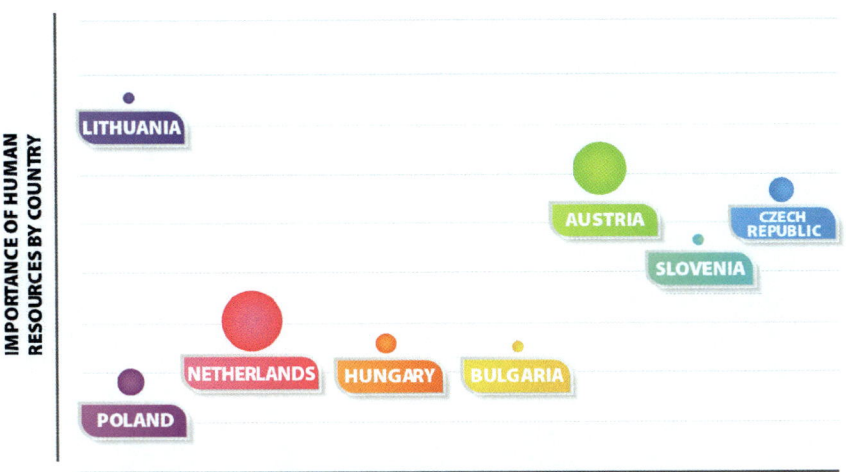

Source: Authors' own elaboration based on national documents and Horizon 2020 Dashboard.

Figure 4.13: Share of the funds attracted under the Horizon 2020 programme

In Figure 4.13, the size of the markers shows the share of funds attracted under Horizon 2020 against the availability of a modern infrastructure and quality HR. The Netherlands and Austria are obvious leaders with the highest share of funds attracted under the Horizon 2020 programme. The most important success factor in those countries is the balance between the significance of the individual indicators. Bulgaria has an extremely low share of funds attracted, and only Lithuania has lower results, but the fact that the latter has a smaller population and respectively a smaller number of researchers than Bulgaria must be taken into account.

Figure 4.14 illustrates the funds attracted under two consecutive Horizon 2020 programmes and the 7th framework programme. The share of funds attracted under the two framework programmes is comparable, and in both cases Austria and the Netherlands once again have the highest share.

IV. Comparing research assessment models on a national level

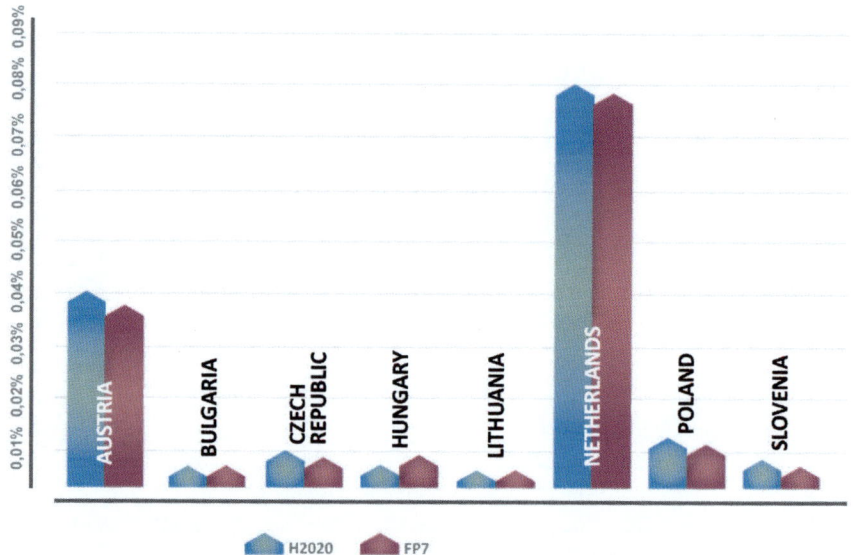

Source: Horizon 2020 Dashboard.

Figure 4.14: Share of the funds attracted under the Horizon 2020 programme and the 7th framework programme

The portfolio of funds attracted is of great importance for a sustainable research system, and a very convincing criterion for a well-functioning system is the size of the funds attracted from the business. The criteria applied in research assessment do not usually take into account the total amount of funds attracted, and only some countries examine the funds attracted per type of source.

Figure 4.15 illustrates the share of funds provided by the business in comparison with the total amount of expenditures for R&D.

4. Main research assessment indicators influencing the innovation ecosystem

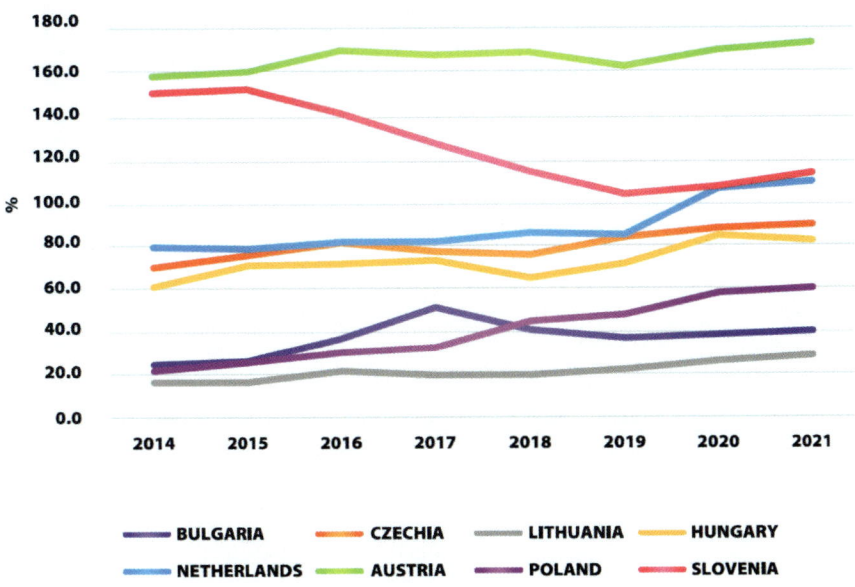

Source: Innovation Scoreboard.

Figure 4.15:   R&D expenditure in the business sector

Austria has the highest share of funds for R&D invested by the business. The percentage of funds is calculated based on the average EU values in 2014, which are accepted as 100 %. An increase is also observed in the Netherlands, while there is a decrease in Slovenia. There is no notable increase in the Czech Republic and Hungary, but a positive trend is observed in regards to the development of the innovation ecosystem. No positive trend is observed in Bulgaria, and the lack of proactivity on the part of the business predetermines the lack of visible intervention on the innovation ecosystem.

IV. Comparing research assessment models on a national level

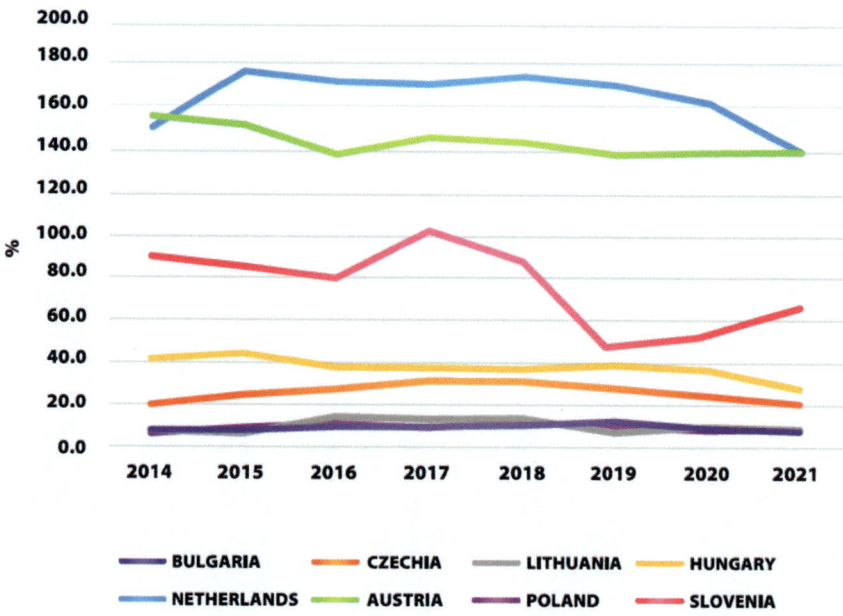

Source: Innovation Scoreboard.

Figure 4.16: PCT patent applications

Figure 4.16 illustrates the percentage of patent applications based on the 2014 EU average values. It is evident that the activity of the new Member States is much lower than that of the Netherlands and Austria. In terms of activity, Slovenia is, to a certain extent, an exception, but over the last three years a decrease and an unstable behaviour with regards to this activity have been observed. Bulgaria, Poland, and Lithuania show the lowest activity. Such results may be due to both a lack of understanding with regards to the management of intellectual property products and a lack of proactivity on the part of SMEs. The lack of incentives for increasing this activity is also an important factor. The legal basis with regards to the storing and management of intellectual products is harmonised and so the reason for the low level of activity in those countries might be due to the low share of R&D investments in the GDP. Inevitably, the lack of dedicated funds for patent application and maintenance further worsens the situation.

5. Participation in partnership networks

One of the signs for the system's research capacity is the participation of individual units in various partnership networks. In several editions of the framework programmes there is a specialised tool called ERA_NET, which stimulates and supports the creation and/or participation in this type of networks. The tool supports only horizontal activities, and the specific research of the participants is a contribution of their countries.

The number of international networks in which each of the countries has participated is illustrated in Table 4.2. It shows only the networks created within the Horizon 2020 programme.

Table 4.2: ERA-NET Partnerships under Funding Programme Horizon 2020

Country	Partnerships
Austria	62
Bulgaria	22
Czech Republic	31
Hungary	31
Lithuania	29
Netherlands	71
Poland	64
Slovenia	39

Source: ERA-Learn, network information, https://www.era-learn.eu/network-information/networks/view.

The Netherlands and Austria are once again the leaders in this respect, while the other countries, with the exception of Poland, have a very low number of participations in networks. Bulgaria has one of the lowest results. This can be explained with the lack of funding for research here (under 1 % of GDP allocated to research) and with the decreased activity of researchers with regards to applying for European financial instruments. The countries which have a similar indicator actually share a similar issue. They should, first of all, increase the competitiveness of their research teams through different approaches; secondly, they should introduce specific incentives for participation in European initiatives (the existence of an increasing number of national instruments which are less competitive considerably reduces the activity of researchers with regards to competing in European initiatives).

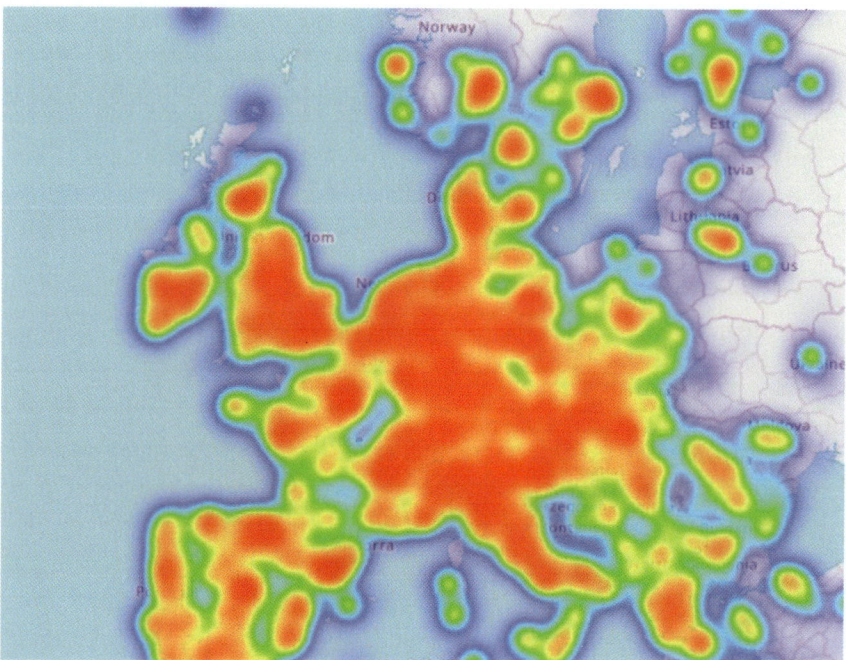

Source: Cordis datalab – Collaboration network, https://cordis.europa.eu/datalab/datalab.php.

Figure 4.17: Partnership networks

The map in Figure 4.17 illustrates the networks established for cooperation between individual organisations. The most saturated zones have a higher number of participants in networks. As regards the countries subject of this study, the Netherlands and Austria are the most active ones, followed by Slovenia, while Poland, Lithuania, and Bulgaria show lower rates of participation.

Those countries which have a well-developed innovation ecosystem do balance their indicators without placing an unnecessary focus on bibliometrics; instead, they emphasise the importance of having a modern research infrastructure, human resources, open science and a broad portfolio of financial income, without it being dominated by public funding. Moreover, if these findings were juxtaposed to the countries' ranking in terms of their innovation profile according to the European Innovation Board, their position would largely confirm the conclusions made above.

Over the past decade, the aim of research assessment has supported the management of research institutions and has ensured clear accountability before the public. According to Jappe (2018), this function has one focus for organisations, where an indicator-based assessment is implemented, and another focus in the process for evaluating researchers. In many cases, when the interpretation of individual indicators according to different disciplines is determined by external sources, such as scientometricians and data providers, the standards for research achievements are not analysed by experts in given fields (Szomszor et al., 2021). As regards research of political or industrial interest, the usability and applicability are assessed, not the academic references. Moed (2005) believes that the analysis of citations clearly distinguishes good and bad studies but is limited with regards to differentiating between good and excellent ones. Citations increase over time and at different rate with regards to individual disciplines, and they are also influenced by cultural specificities (Szomszor et al., 2021). In most cases, the research assessment pays attention to research achievements, which in turn depend on the context in which they are studied (Nature, 2018). The indicators for novelty and usability of research also vary, but they can be perceived in a very different way.

The entities implementing the research assessment should take into account the levels of international cooperation, the impact of local factors, national specifics, and cultural traditions, and the analysis must include a full set of data, not just momentary metrics (Szomszor et al., 2021). The Institute for Scientific Information (https://clarivate.com/webofsciencegroup/solutions/isi-institute-for-scientific-information/) relies on indicators such as public expenses for research, patents, publications, citations, open access, and the existence of an active international cooperation (Adams & Rogers, 2021).

References

Academy of Agricultural Sciences Act, https://www.lex.bg/laws/ldoc/2134696961

Act on the Bulgarian Academy of Sciences, https://www.lex.bg/laws/ldoc/2132584961

Adams, J., & Rogers, G. (2021). *The Annual G20 Scorecard – Research Performance 2021*. Institute for scientific information, https://clarivate.com/lp/the-annual-g20-scorecard-research-performance-2021/

Arnold, E., & Mahieu, B. (2015). *R&D Evaluation Methodology and Funding Principles: Summary Report*. Technopolis Group, https://www.technopolis-group.com/wp-content/uploads/2020/02/Reform-of-the-research-assessment-and-institutional-funding-system-in-the-Czech-Republic.pdf

Austrian Platform for Research and Technology Policy Evaluation, https://fteval.at/

Austrian Platform for Research and Technology Policy Evaluation (2019). *Evaluation Standards in Research, Technology and Innovation Policy*. Vienna. DOI: 10.22163/fteval.2019.344

Broek-Honingh, N. G., van den Koens, L., & Vennekens, A. (2020). *Totale Investeringen in Wetenschap en Innovatie 2018–2024*. Den Haag: Rathenau Instituut, https://www.rathenau.nl/sites/default/files/2020-04/TWIN-rapport%202018-2024.pdf

Cornell University, INSEAD & WIPO (2020). *The Global Innovation Index 2020: Who Will Finance Innovation?* Ithaca, Fontainebleau, Geneva, https://globalinnovationindex.org/

Council for Research, Development and Innovation (2019). *Innovation Strategy of the Czech Republic 2019–2030*. Office of the Government of the Czech Republic, https://www.vyzkum.cz/FrontClanek.aspx?idsekce=867922

Csomos, G. (2021). *A critical review of the proposed reforms of the academic performance indicators applied in the assessment of researchers' performance in Hungary*. Retrieved February 13, 2022 from the arXiv database. arXiv:2110.13459

Détourbe, M. A. (2016). From Public Funding to Public Investment in Research: A Study of Research Funding Policies and their Impact through two Research Assessment Campaigns in the United Kingdom. *Revue LISA/LISA e-journal*, 14 (1) [Online]. DOI: https://doi.org/10.4000/lisa.8903

Dichev, I. (2020). Zashto Bulgaria nyama top universiteti (Why Bulgaria does not have top universities). *DW*, https://p.dw.com/p/3eN4O

Ecker, B., Brunner, P., Christmann-Budian, S., Fischl, I., Gassler, H., Gogola, G., Hartmann, E., Heckl, E., Kaufmann, P., Krabel, S., Mayer, K., Mozhova, A., Pechar, H., Radauer, A., Reiner, C., Ruhland, S., Sardadvar, S., Schneider, H. W., Schuch, K., Sturn, D., Tiefenthaler, B., Warta, K., & Welp-Park, E. (2019). *Austrian Research and Technology Report 2019*. Federal Ministry of Education, Science, and Research, Federal Ministry for Transport, Innovation, and Technology, Federal Ministry for Digital and Economic Affairs, https://www.zsi.at/object/publication/5340/attach/Austrian_Research_and_Technology_Report_2019.pdf

Ecker, B., Reiner, C., & Gogola, G. (2017). *HEInnovate in Austria: Background report*. WPZ Research GmbH, www.bmbwf.gv.at

Economic and Social Research Council, https://esrc.ukri.org/

Eisenhut, T. (2020). The regional research policy of the Austrian federal states. *Central European Economic Journal*, 7 (54), 227–241, https://doi.org/10.2478/ceej-2020-0012

Euraxess Poland, https://www.euraxess.pl/

European Commission (2015). Preissler, S., Mahr, A., Henriques, L., et al. *Peer review of the Bulgarian research and innovation system: Horizon 2020 policy support facility*. Publications Office, https://data.europa.eu/doi/10.2777/17938

European Commission, Directorate-General for Research and Innovation (2016). *Peer Review of the Hungarian Research and Innovation system*. Publications Office of the European Union. DOI: 10.2777/236994, https://rio.jrc.ec.europa.eu/library/peer-review-hungarian-research-and-innovation-system

European Commission, Directorate-General for Research and Innovation (2017). *Peer Review of Poland's Higher Education and Science System*. Publications Office of the European Union. DOI: 0.2777/193011, https://rio.jrc.ec.europa.eu/sites/default/files/report/PSF-Peer_review_Poland_FINAL%20REPORT.pdf

Eurydice, https://eacea.ec.europa.eu/national-policies/eurydice

Federal Ministry of Education, Science, and Research. (2018). *Austrian National Development Plan for Public Universities 2019–2024*. Vienna, https://bmbwf.gv.at/wissenschaft-hochschulen/universitaeten/der-gesamtoesterreichische-universitaetsentwicklungsplan-2019-2024/

Fonds zur Förderung der wissenschaftlichen Forschung. *Evaluation in the FWF*, https://m.fwf.ac.at/fileadmin/files/Dokumente/Entscheidung_Evaluation/EN_evaluation-fwf/evaluation-en_fwf.pdf

Global Incubator Network Austria (GIN), https://www.gin-austria.com/

Good, B., Vermeulen, N., Tiefenthaler, B., & Arnold, E. (2015). Counting quality? The Czech performance-based research funding system. *Research Evaluation*, 24 (2), 91–105, https://doi.org/10.1093/reseval/rvu035

Government Strategic Analysis Centre (Lithuania) – Strata, https://strata.gov.lt/en/

Hasprová, O., Brabec, Z., & Rozkovec, J. (2018). Intangible assets disclosed by public universities in Czech Republic. *Journal of International Studies*, 11 (1), 67–79. DOI: 10.14254/2071-8330.2018/11-1/5, https://www.jois.eu/files/5_303_Hasprova%20et%20al.pdf

Higher Education and Research Act (Netherlands), https://wetten.overheid.nl/BWBR0005682/2021-01-01

Hojnik, J. (2019). Evaluation of academic legal publications in Slovenia. *Evaluating Academic Legal Research in Europe*, 341–383. DOI: 10.4337/9781788115506.00017

Hollanders, H. (2020). *European Innovation Scoreboard 2020 as part of the European Innovation Scoreboards (EIS) project*. Luxembourg: Publications Office of the EU, https://ec.europa.eu/docsroom/documents/42981

Jappe, A., Pithan, D., & Heinze, T. (2018). Does bibliometric research confer legitimacy to research assessment practice? A sociological study of reputational control, 1972–2016. *PloS One 13*, e0199031. DOI: 10.1371/journal.pone.0199031

Johnston, R. (2008) On Structuring Subjective Judgements: Originality, Significance and Rigour in RAE 2008. *Higher Education Quarterly*, 62 (1–2), 120–147

Korytkowski, P., & Kulczycki, E. (2019). Examining how country-level science policy shapes publication patterns: the case of Poland. *Scientometrics*, 119 (3), 1519–1543, https://doi.org/10.1007/s11192-019-03092-1

Kulczycki, E., Korzeń, M., & Korytkowski, P. (2017). Toward an excellence-based research funding system: Evidence from Poland. *Journal of Informetrics*, 11 (1), 282–298, https://doi.org/10.1016/j.joi.2017.01.001

Kulczycki, E., Rozkosz, E. A., Szadkowski, K., Ciereszko, K., Hołowiecki, M., & Krawczyk, F. (2020). Local use of metrics for the research assessment of academics: the case of Poland. *Journal of Higher Education Policy and Management.* DOI: 10.1080/1360080X.2020.1846243

Lucas, L. (2006). *The Research Game in Academic Life.* Maidenhead: Open University Press & Society for Research into Higher Education.

Methodology for assessing applications to invitations. Slovenian Research Agency, https://www.arrs.si/en/akti/metod-skupna-12.asp?ZaTisk=Da

Moed, H. F. (2005). *Citation analysis in research evaluation.* Dordrecht, Netherlands: Springer.

Moldicz, C. (2020). Hungary economy briefing: Science and technology innovation mechanisms in Hungary. *China-CEE Institute*, 32 (2), https://china-cee.eu/2020/09/18/hungary-economy-briefing-science-and-technology-innovation-mechanisms-in-hungary/

Naredba za usloviyata i reda za otsenkata, planiraneto, razpredelenieto i razhodvaneto na sredstvata ot darzhavnia byudzhet za finansirane na prisashtata na darzhavnite visshi uchilishta nauchna ili hudozhestvenotvorcheska deynost (Ordinance on the conditions and procedure for assessment, planning, allocation and spending of the funds of the state budget for the purpose of financing the ordinary research or artistic activity of state higher education institutions), https://www.mon.bg/bg/59

National Innovation Office (2014). National Smart Specialisation Strategy, https://nkfih.gov.hu/english-2017/strategy-making-by-the/strategic-documents

National Research, Development, and Innovation Office, https://nkfih.gov.hu/about-the-office

National Science Centre, Poland, https://ncn.gov.pl/en/

National Science Fund (NSF), Bulgaria, https://www.fni.bg/

Natsionalnata strategia za razvitie na nauchnite izsledvania v Republika Bulgaria, 2017–2030 (2017–2030 National Research Development Strategy of the Republic of Bulgaria), https://www.mon.bg/bg/143

Nature (2018). Science needs to redefine excellence: the concept of research excellence is ubiquitous, but its meaning depends on context (editorial). *Nature*, 554, 403–404. DOI: 10.1038/d41586-018-02183-y

Netherlands Code of Conduct for Research Integrity, https://www.vsnu.nl/files/documents/Netherlands%20Code%20of%20Conduct%20for%20Research%20Integrity%202018.pdf

Netherlands Organisation for Scientific Research (2018). *Connecting Science and Society, NWO strategy 2019-2022.* Hague, https://www.nwo.nl/sites/nwo/files/documents/NWO_strategy_2019-2022_Connecting_Science_and_Society.pdf

OECD & European Union (2019). *Supporting Entrepreneurship and Innovation in Higher Education in Austria.* OECD Skills Studies. Paris: OECD Publishing, https://doi.org/10.1787/1c45127b-en

Office of the Government of the Czech Republic (2018). *Methodology for Evaluating Research Organisations in the University Sector.* Government of the Czech Republic.

Order on the Adoption of The Annual Regulation on Research and Experimental Development and Evaluation of Artistic Activities by Universities and Research Institutes, https://www.e-tar.lt/portal/en/legalAct/69270ef0a8d411e78a4c904b1afa0332

Petersohn, S., Biesenbender, S., & Thiedig, C. (2020). Investigating Assessment Standards in the Netherlands, Italy, and the United Kingdom: Challenges for Responsible Research Evaluation. *Shaping the Future Through Standardization*. IGI Global. DOI: 10.4018/978-1-7998-2181-6.ch003

Plamenov, P. (2017). Ecstasy and Trembling, or On the Inner Mobility of the Aesthetical. *Philosophical Alternatives*, 2017/4, 116–129.

Polish National Agency for Academic Exchange, https://nawa.gov.pl/en

Research Excellence Framework, https://www.ref.ac.uk/

Research, Development, and Innovation Council Department (2018). *Methodology for Evaluating Research Organisations and Research, Development and Innovation Purpose-Tied Aid Programmes*. Office of the Government of the Czech Republic, https://www.vyzkum.cz/FrontClanek.aspx?idsekce=695512

Rules on the Procedures for the (Co)financing and Assessment of Research Activities and on Monitoring the Implementation of Research Activities. Slovenian Research Agency, https://www.arrs.si/en/akti/20/prav-sof-ocen-sprem-razisk-dej-okt20.asp

Saenen, B., & Borrell-Damián, L. (2019). *EUA Briefing: Reflections on University Research Assessment – Key concepts, issues and actors*. European University Association, Brussels, https://eua.eu/downloads/publications/reflections%20on%20university%20research%20assessment%20key%20concepts%20issues%20and%20actors.pdf

Science Europe (2020). *Position Statement and Recommendations on Research Assessment Processes*. Science Europe AISBL, Brussels, https://www.scienceeurope.org/media/3twjxim0/se-position-statement-research-assessment-processes.pdf

Scientific Research Promotion Act, Bulgaria, https://www.lex.bg/laws/ldoc/2135472978

Slovenian Research Agency, https://www.arrs.si/en/

State agency CzechInvest, http://www.czech-research.com/

Sturn, D., Dall, E., Degelsegger-Márquez, A., Lampert, D., & Schuch, K. (2018). Zwischenevaluierung des Programms "Beyond Europe" (Interim evaluation of the Program "Beyond Europe"). Vienna, https://www.zsi.at/de/object/publication/5158

Szomszor, M., Adams, J. Fry, R., Gebert, C., Pendlebury, D. A., Potter, R. W., & Rogers, G. (2021). Interpreting Bibliometric Data. *Frontiers in Research Metric Analysis*, https://doi.org/10.3389/frma.2020.628703

Technopolis Group, https://www.technopolis-group.com/

The Austrian Research Promotion Agency (FFG), https://www.ffg.at/en/FFG/The-FFG

The Royal Netherlands Academy of Arts and Sciences (KNAW), https://www.knaw.nl/en

VSNU, KNAW & NOW (2020). *The Strategy Evaluation Protocol 2021–2027 – SEP*. Hague, https://www.vsnu.nl/files/documenten/Domeinen/Onderzoek/SEP_2021-2027.pdf

Vutsova, A., Arabadzhieva, M., & Hristov, T. (2021). Impact assessment of research evaluation in Bulgaria. *COLLNET Journal of Scientometrics and Information Management*. DOI: 10.1080/09737766.2021.1962767

Website of the Republic of Poland, https://www.gov.pl/

Witty, A. (2013). *Encouraging a British invention revolution: Sir Andrew Witty's review of universities and growth.* https://www.gov.uk/government/uploads/system/uploads/attachment_data/file/249720/bis-13-1241-encouraging-a-british-invention-revolution-andrew-witty-review-R1.pdf

V. Concluding reflection and forward looking

The book provides a reflection on research assessment – what it is, why it is being carried out and who is performing it, in an attempt to understand how to best implement it. As it could be expected, we do not advocate one single way of conducting research evaluation and assessment. The excellence in the title should be regarded rather as kaizen, or continuous improvement of the way we comprehend and organise research endeavours, than a final blueprint.

We also argue that the excellent research assessment should contribute towards assisting the nexus of research stakeholders to reach a dynamic consensus on how to spend limited public resources towards the end of having plausible new scientific discoveries, solve pressing societal and business problems and create sustainable wealth.

We believe the current time calls for a reset and a reimagining of research evaluation activities, keeping the lessons learnt from the past in mind and looking forward to a new economic world. As of today, research evaluation is an immanent part of research policy and political priorities. However, we might want to see research evaluation as a complimentary self-reflection for the academia itself.

By shifting the focus from the (research) outcomes towards the process (of research discovery) we might be able to bring research evaluation to kaizen. Embedding innovative experimental participative forms of assessment, will certainly change the general picture of the assessment process and the system will become more flexible whilst losing some of its rigidity and bureaucracy.

A lot of researchers doubt whether the current governance of research lead to "higher quality" of research (Grande et al, 2013; Finke, 2014). Concerns are related even with the very "holy grail" of the current academic publishing – the "double blind review". It often limits the academic dispute "behind closed doors" and influences the research production through the researcher expectation of publishability of results, rather than their genuine academic judgement. The very academic process is outcome-oriented, rather than process-oriented and hence the research evaluation systems tend to replicate that. Often even the conferences are judged rather on if their proceedings are indexed in Web of Science or Scopus and not on what debate would happen there. Book projects usually provide greater flexibility, yet not all universities favour them for academic progress.

We conducted a comprehensive comparative analysis of research evaluation practices and their interdependence with the national innovation ecosystem in eight European Union countries. By doing so, we wanted to understand how the existing institutions frame research assessment systems and whether there is a difference in utilizing them as a political control mechanism (Shore & Wright, 1999), and whether this improves the output quality of the research system.

We employed a holistic approach in the study and a multi-vector (or multi-functional) system in order to present the research evaluation systems in the selected countries, and analysed their specific impact on the innovation ecosystem. To a certain extent the novelty in our approach allowed us to reach the conclusion that research evaluation is indeed used as a control mechanism, but not by the policymakers, but rather by the internal (to the universities) power networks. These networks are usually well-balanced and external (to the universities) reforms happen rarely. These reforms are most often internalised differently depending on which network is in power. This difference is higher in countries with lower law-enforcement.

We argued that research assessment should be considered within a managerial, economic, social, and environmental sustainability. A metaphor which helps us grasp the role of research assessment in the academic landscape is *gravity*. It dominates and governs research behaviour. It is conservative and preserves the status-quo in the long-run. Thus, a lot of progressive researchers are critical towards research assessment systems as they serve as additional gravity-centres and prevent quick changes sought by them – i.e., decoupling the academic career from the lengthy and expensive publishing process, democratizing the higher education process in a manner similar to the secondary education in Finland or, for example, in public schools in Maryland, USA. Progressive researchers would seek reforms, which will decrease inequality among universities and research centres originating from funding based on expensive publications.

Gravity, at the same time, helps organize chaos. In post-socialist societies the newly adopted research assessment systems, which mimic European models, served as a transformative power – dispose of the old gurus, who were gravitating around old, centralized models or at least change their orbit to have a western focus. At the same time, local systems were already conservative, so they responded by negotiating with the major reference databases to include local outlets as well.

Countries like Austria and the Netherlands (or more generally those with traditions in market economy, democracy and civil society development) would tend to be more holistic and include criteria such as sustainable economic development, societal relevance, and viability in their research assessments (on every level: institutional, regional, or national). The holistic approach would require the involvement of civil society, and research performance would be evaluated also against the user's satisfaction (of research results). Holistic gravity tends to have strange attractors and less chaos and anomalies (for more details of chaos theory metaphors in management see Gilstrap, 2005).

By contrast, the new member states tend to focus on the abstract value of research measured by quantitative indicators related to publications only. Poland differs from the other CEEs by being closer to the holistic countries. In the book we discussed various potential explanations of those observations, among them the overall implementation of the rule of law or the lack of coherent industry-academia partnerships. Moreover, the distinction in the degree of holisticness could be attributed to the differences in participatory engagement of the overall policymaking. Last but not least, research assessment is both an instrument of control within the academic institution and it is also being shaped by the overall governance of academic institutions.

Countries and institutions which rely substantively on the whole Web of Science and Scopus and prioritize only quantitative indicators tend to produce more chaos, since gravity-centres emerge randomly and generate anomalies (i.e. researchers with relatively high scientometrics – close to 100 publications in Web of Science and Hirsch index=7, several doctoral degrees and professorships and at the same time – widely used plagiarism as a publication strategy and low overall quality of publications). Top universities in Germany and the UK for instance, maintain their own lists of recommended journals as publication outlets, quite shorter than the respective WoS/Scopus lists. The local conservative research community found easy strategies to publish a lot in the sacral databases without much impact or even negotiated cross-reference, which would be a proxy for impact.

Research evaluation as a holistic endeavour with a structured mix of different activities incorporates non-typical scientific activities which, however, are an immanent part of the research process itself. Such activities include communication with different stakeholders, including societal, political, and the media. Thus, we did the same – we talked to policymakers, researchers, NGO activists, science communicators, and journalists. We found a great deal of dialectics in terms of which indicators signals what in different contexts.

Research evaluation could and should serve as a basis for a redesign of policies, if necessary, and increase research accountability to society. Last but not least, it provides legitimization for the resources invested. In this sense, its intervention in the innovation system could be quite tangible and could normatively contribute to its improvement. However, in certain cases the research evaluation system creates incentives for those involved to focus on its maintenance and reiteration, rather than on achieving kaizen.

So, in principle effective research evaluation and assessment should contribute to a higher level of coherence of research programmes, research performance, and societal impact. There is no clear high level of coherence in new member states due to the fact that the holistic approach in research evaluation is not used by them. One of the reasons for that could be fragmented and incomplete national innovation ecosystems consisting of smaller sub-ecosystems where stakeholders form isolated cliques instead of interlocking dense networks.

The German system of career development through various universities provide an excellent interlocking governance, but it is unclear how we could transform one system (shorter pre-career periods, inbreeding, high share of tenured lecturers, difficult lay-offs, low basic salary with virtually no performance based payment, commercialising reputation in business or projects) into another (longer and more diversified academic paths, high diversity in payment, high share of non-tenured lecturers and assistants, performance based requirements).

If we do want to change the way research evaluations work and impact the strategic planning of research organisations, we might want to involve the new generation of researchers who are still not burdened by traditions or historical overlays. Revolutionary changes always come from the young. They can change the rigidity of the system, make it future-oriented, and engage more and new stakeholders and channel their value propositions towards the research system. Attracting new stakeholders into the evaluation process will cease its momentous performance because the quality and impact of the research evaluation process depends not only on the main performers but also on all supporting staff involved in the process and on the audience, which should be adequately preluded in advance. We could talk about evaluation curators from the early stage of preparation of the evaluation. The same way as curators redefine art and add value to the exhibition or performance, those research evaluation curators could be the masters of this collective priority-setting mechanism. Using the 12 art roles (Kolev, 2023) we can enrich the assessment stakeholder diversity by instrumenting the patron (companies), connoisseur (anti-plagiarism technologies) and others.

Activities related to research assessment have an impact on the development of the innovation ecosystem. In some cases, the intervention is effective and leads to a clear positive development trend. In other cases, the intervention is more sporadic, and this does not lead to the anticipated effect on the innovation ecosystem.

An important factor for the lack of coherence between research programs, research performance and societal impact in Eastern European countries is the strong insider influence on how the external research evaluation programs are internalized. While in Western academic landscapes we can partially accept the criticism of audit culture by Shore & Wright (1999), in Eastern academic landscapes and Bulgaria in particular, the research evaluation systems favour inertia.

In order to enhance the overall effect of the impact on the innovation ecosystem, the research assessment criteria system should be changed in two aspects: reviewing/bringing main indicators up-to-date and introducing adequate impacts for the individual criteria. Also, it is possible to create a criteria system which is similar to the ones in other countries where there are two types of indicators: compulsory and additional. Each of these groups deals with specific impacts relevant to the potential impact of a given indicator.

The research assessment has to be conducted based on the highest ethical standards and in good faith both on the part of the assessors and the entities providing the information for the assessment, in order to guarantee the usefulness of this specific activity for the units which are being assessed and the policymakers. Ethical standards should be inherently linked to a clear guarantee for lack of plagiarism.

For the purpose of improving the innovation ecosystem, it is necessary to monitor and control the assessment processes and their impact on quality by taking into consideration the interests of the stakeholders and by maintaining an open dialogue with them.

As we live in turbulent times, the research institutions at all levels – department, organisation, regional or national level – should be ready to react to external shocks. First, we have had to face various crises – Covid-19, extreme floods, Russia-Ukraine war and so on. Despite the existence of various scenarios for all such events, the research systems must quickly adapt, study, and propose advice in a fundamentally shorter timeframe than before. Second, universities and research organisations should behave as they are teaching and preaching; they should be more environmentally-friendly, socially-responsible, and open to societal problems the same way as they are open to business problems. So, research evaluation systems should be able to capture the research impact along those criteria as well.

Based on the analysis, we could derive the following three key principles in research evaluation, which are prerequisites for quality and impactful research evaluation leading to research excellence:

- transparency: sharing the preparatory work, progress performance and results;
- collaboration: intertwining research and societal stakeholders and policy processes;
- trust and integrity: enhancing the academic reputation and maintaining integrity of research evaluation processes.

The Eastern European transition towards market economies used significantly the newly formed civil society organisations. They experienced different influence – predominately the Anglo-Saxon way of organisation of civil society, however Germany, Netherlands and Austria also shaped them. The German political foundations resorted to supporting civil society in doing socially important research, rather than the universities. So, politically the Eastern European civil society has enough foreign reputation (not to mention in US and UK) to be included as a valuable stakeholder in the next generation research evaluation. Ironically, often development projects of civil society organisations led to academic publications. Independent researchers contributed to citizen science of higher international impact (number of publications, academic citations and reference in policy documents) even compared to top schools of social science in some countries.

We would outline the following observations for the system:

The periodic research assessment does not have a clear effect on the innovation ecosystem. Some elements thereof are implemented but no tangible positive and sustainable trend can be established. The elements influenced by the implementation of research assessment can be found in:

- different levels of steady internationalisation of research and its presence in international research networks;
- ambitions to increase participation in research projects- national and international with a different scope. This is a clear sign that the project culture, capacity and competitiveness of the research and innovation potential is increasing;
- research training of PhD students which practically leads to an improvement in the quality of the staff.

Based on the analysis, we could project that it is highly advisable for other small countries on the Balkans (they are either accession countries or in pre-accession status) to introduce an independent external assessment of the research system for a given period of time. In this respect, the past practices – albeit sporadic – confirm the usefulness of this type of assessment.

Subject to discussion is, however, to what extent findings of this kind will be taken into account and will be followed up by corrective actions for the purpose of filling the gaps in the system. The practice in other countries is varied, but in those cases where the national structures have followed the recommendations and have undertaken the relevant actions, the effect on the innovation ecosystem is tangible. In those cases where the recommendations are ignored, there is no change in the existing status of the innovation ecosystem.

The literature review identified various studies of the future of research evaluation. It is extremely quantitative, dominated by smarter and more intelligent bibliometric infrastructure (Krüger & Petersohn, 2022) and new alternative metrics, including text mining and integrated open data on which research is based (Wilsdon et al, 2017). Media-driven rankings such as Handelsblatt BWL ranking and Times Higher Education will continue to emerge and contribute towards the reputation of the universities and their research. Yet, what is missing in the existing visions of future research evaluation is its perception as an epistemic process in the context of different epistemic regimes (Böschen, 2019), which is also a collective priority-setting mechanism.

We also offer a rather eccentric proposal – gamification of research evaluation with a variable term for periodic assessments or a continuous assessment and participation of all different stakeholders – academia, business, civil society, and policymakers. After all, the research evaluation is a game of reputation, and we should employ techniques that effectively govern gamification. In recent years the monopoly of academic researchers over the "academic knowledge" has been dissolved by having a lot of civil society activists, business experts and even policymakers publishing through the "double blind review" process in reputable outlets. So, research evaluation should be extended towards the whole ecosystem producing *knowledge* and engaging all of those, who produce and consume knowledge. If we want a democratising science we need to have a democratised research evaluation system.

Institutions like the National Science Foundation, the Joint Research Center of the European Commission, Max Plank Society and the Chinese Academy of Sciences have already experimented with artificial intelligence tools for scientific assessments. Definitely AI would attract significant attention of research assessment scholars in the future!

References:

Böschen, S. (2019). Processing issues in science policy: Emerging epistemic regimes. In *Handbook on science and public policy* (pp. 317–335). Edward Elgar Publishing.

Gilstrap, D. L. (2005). Strange attractors and human interaction: Leading complex organisations through the use of metaphors.

Grande, E., Jansen, D., Jarren, O., Rip, A., Schimank, U., & Weingart, P. (eds). (2013). *Neue Governance der Wissenschaft: Reorganisation-externe Anforderungen-Medialisierung.* transcript Verlag.

Finke, P. (2014). Citizen science. *Das unterschätzte Wissen der Laien. München: oekom.*

Kolev, I. (2023). Defining art as phenomenal being. *Arts* 12:100

Krüger, A. K., & Petersohn, S. (2022). From Research Evaluation to Research Analytics. The digitization of academic performance measurement. *Valuation Studies, 9*(1), 11–46.

Shore, C., & Wright, S. (1999). Audit culture and anthropology: Neo-liberalism in British higher education. *Journal of the royal anthropological institute,* 557–575.

Wilsdon, J. R., Bar-Ilan, J., Frodeman, R., Lex, E., Peters, I., & Wouters, P. (2017). Next-generation metrics: Responsible metrics and evaluation for open science.

List of authors

Vutsova, Albena

Albena Vutsova is a professor at the Faculty of Economics and Business Administration, Sofia University "St. Kliment Ohridski", Bulgaria. She conducts research and publishes in monitoring, analysis and effectiveness of educational, scientific and innovative activities. She has participated in more than 40 international projects over the past 10 years. Prof. Vutsova has 12 PhD graduates under her guidance.

Albena has 20 years of professional experience in the development and implementation of targeted policies in science and higher education; in the management of national and European programs and projects in the field of education and science. She has been part of international teams for the development of educational and scientific policies for candidate countries for EU membership (Ukraine, Serbia, Kosovo, Bosnia and Herzegovina). She is also an evaluator of scientific projects for national and international financial instruments (Framework programs for science, technological development and innovation; International doctoral schools, Fulbright Program, COST Program, etc.). She is a member of the ENRESSH Network, AESIS Network.

Prof. Vutsova is a member of the Board of Governors of the Joint Research Center (JRC) of the European Commission, as well as member of various working groups within DG Research.

Yalamov, Todor

Todor Yalamov is an Associate Professor and Vice Dean for Research, Innovation and Projects at the Faculty of Economics and Business Administration (FEBA), Sofia University "St. Kliment Ohridski", Bulgaria and Professor at the Faculty of Business Administration, Soka University, Tokyo, Japan. Todor's research interests include corporate governance, anticorruption, innovation and knowledge economy, gamification, and entrepreneurship. He is the academic director of the MBA program in Strategic Management at Sofia University.

Prof. Yalamov was a Fulbright scholar at the Center for International Private Enterprise in Washington, DC and worked as a senior analyst for the Center for the Study of Democracy, Bulgaria. Todor has a long track-record in providing incubation and entrepreneurship support services in Bulgaria and Eastern Europe and Central Asia.

Arabadzhieva, Martina

Dr. Martina Arabadzhieva is a chief assistant professor at the Faculty of Economics and Business Administration, Sofia University "Kliment Ohridski", Bulgaria. Her research interests are related to the study of research evaluation, financial management of higher education, social entrepreneurship, and youth unemployment. Martina serves as a consultant to scientific journals, working with global research databases, works on various national and international projects dedicated to education and science, and has a prior experience in the field of human resources.

Martina has been trained in a Fulbright course for project management and evaluation and is certified Project Management Professional by the Project Management Institute, USA. Her project activities include work under the European programs Erasmus +, Horizon 2020, Marie Skłodowska Curie, the European Scientific Council, COST program, as well as a number of national programs.

Dr. Arabadzhieva is part of the AESIS Network for Advancing & Evaluating the Societal Impact of Science and has published in indexed national and international journals.